MW01712164

PENGUIN CANADA

BUILDING THE BEST

ANTHONY GRNAK, Deloitte partner, has helped private and public companies transform themselves into successful organizations. He has held a leadership role with Canada's 50 Best Managed Companies program for ten years. He lives in Toronto.

JOHN HUGHES, Deloitte partner, has spent twenty years helping entrepreneurs and has played a leadership role in Canada's 50 Best Managed Companies program since its inception. He lives in Toronto.

DOUGLAS HUNTER has written widely on business, history, and sport. He is the author of several books, including *Open Ice*; *War Games*; *Molson: The Birth of a Business Empire*; *Glory Barons*; and most recently, *The Bubble and the Bear: How Nortel Burst the Canadian Dream*, which won the National Business Book Award. He lives on Severn Sound in Georgian Bay.

BUILDING THE BEST

Lessons from Inside Canada's Best Managed Companies

ANTHONY GRNAK, JOHN HUGHES, AND DOUGLAS HUNTER

PENGUIN
CANADA

PENGUIN CANADA

Published by the Penguin Group

Penguin Group (Canada), 90 Eglinton Avenue East, Suite 700, Toronto, Ontario, Canada M4P 2Y3 (a division of Pearson Canada Inc.)

Penguin Group (USA) Inc., 375 Hudson Street, New York, New York 10014, U.S.A.
Penguin Books Ltd, 80 Strand, London WC2R 0RL, England
Penguin Ireland, 25 St Stephen's Green, Dublin 2, Ireland (a division of Penguin Books Ltd)
Penguin Group (Australia), 250 Camberwell Road, Camberwell, Victoria 3124, Australia (a division of Pearson Australia Group Pty Ltd)
Penguin Books India Pvt Ltd, 11 Community Centre, Panchsheel Park, New Delhi – 110 017, India
Penguin Group (NZ), cnr Airborne and Rosedale Roads, Albany, Auckland 1310, New Zealand (a division of Pearson New Zealand Ltd)
Penguin Books (South Africa) (Pty) Ltd, 24 Sturdee Avenue, Rosebank, Johannesburg 2196, South Africa

Penguin Books Ltd, Registered Offices: 80 Strand, London WC2R 0RL, England

First published in a Viking Canada hardcover by Penguin Group (Canada), a division of Pearson Canada Inc., 2006
Published in this edition, 2006

(WEB) 10 9 8 7 6 5 4 3 2 1

Manufactured in Canada.

ISBN-10: 0-14-305111-3
ISBN-13: 978-0-14-305111-4

Library and Archives Canada Cataloguing in Publication data available upon request.

Contents

About Canada's 50 Best Managed Companies Program vii
Foreword xi
Introduction xiii

Strategy

1 Ripe opportunities
Developing an executable strategy to achieve sustainable growth
MAGNOTTA WINERY **3**

2 Learning to play with others
Pursuing and managing alliances, acquisitions, and other strategic relationships
SPIN MASTER **24**

3 Getting the ingredients right
Managing the risks associated with growth
BOSTON PIZZA **52**

Capability

4 Beyond bricks and mortar
Capitalizing on technology solutions
ELLISDON **81**

5 Service, tailormade
Building and sustaining a customer-focused approach to sales and marketing
HARRY ROSEN **99**

6 Moving in all the right directions
Developing and leveraging core competencies
ARMOUR TRANSPORTATION SYSTEMS 122

7 Booming through the bust
Attracting capital and managing finances
MEDIAGRIF INTERACTIVE TECHNOLOGIES 140

8 Laying solid foundations
Designing the right organization and processes to support growth
PCL CONSTRUCTION GROUP OF COMPANIES 162

Commitment

9 Building a better circus
Creating the right leadership and communicating the vision
CIRQUE DU SOLEIL 185

10 Hire learning
Attracting and retaining talent to build an exceptional culture
NATIONAL LEASING 211

Index 235

About Canada's 50 Best Managed Companies Program

Since 1993, the annual Canada's 50 Best Managed Companies awards program has been recognizing top-performing enterprises through an evaluation process that extends well beyond raw financial results. It is unique in the emphasis it places on a broad range of management capabilities, and recognizes a company as a whole, not just senior executives. Currently it is sponsored by Deloitte & Touche LLP, CIBC Commercial Banking, the *National Post,* and Queen's School of Business.

Companies can apply for consideration themselves or be nominated by others; in either case, the companies that do make the annual list of Canada's Best Managed Companies must proceed through a rigorous business review and then pass muster before a panel of judges.

Current standards for consideration in the Phase I portion of the program are:

- revenues greater than $10 million
- superior results for the past three years (e.g., profitability, growth)
- limited to Canadian-owned, closely held (generally less than one hundred shareholders) private companies, including those

controlled by Canadian venture capital and private equity firms *or* Canadian-owned public companies or income trusts with fewer than 50 percent of their shares or units traded

Candidates in Phase I are screened by a panel of Deloitte and CIBC Commercial Banking leaders, who provide independent judgment. Candidates that proceed to Phase II often have the opportunity to meet with a "coach" from Deloitte and CIBC Commercial Banking to aid them in completing the detailed evaluation of their operations based in the areas of strategy, capability, and commitment. Financial performance is also assessed.

The detailed assessment and interviews with the awards program coaches for Phase II are then submitted to the final judging panel. For the most recent awards, this panel consisted of the following:

Russ Robertson joined Deloitte as vice-chairman in June 2002. Russ has thirty-three years of experience with the financial services industry, and was named an FCA in 2002. He is also involved with community organizations such as Junior Achievement, the National Ballet of Canada, and the Schulich School of Business.

Frances McIsaac is vice-president of Strategy and Business Development with CIBC Commercial Banking. She joined CIBC in March 2000 after having held progressively senior positions in the financial services industry. Frances is a graduate of St. Michael's College at the University of Toronto.

Jonathan Harris, executive editor of the *National Post,* joined the newspaper in 2000. He began his professional career at *Maclean's* magazine and then moved on to *Canadian Business* in 1997. That year, he was nominated for a National Magazine

Award for his article on the relationship between high mutual fund fees and poor performance.

Ken Wong is a faculty member at Queen's School of Business, where he has held both teaching and administrative positions. Ken was the principal architect of Queen's MBA for Science & Technology program, was a 1998 winner of the *Financial Post*'s Leaders in Management Education award for his work in Queen's undergraduate commerce, MBA, and executive development programs, and is a frequent speaker at conferences and executive development programs around the world. In 2005, Ken was named the Queen's Commerce '77 Teaching Fellow in Marketing, and is a 2006 inductee into the Canadian Marketing Hall of Legends.

The program's judges select the fifty winners, which are unranked. These include new applicants as well as companies that qualify to retain the designation as a Best Managed Company. After having been selected once, winners can remain on the Best Managed list for up to two more years by proceeding through a requalification process. After that, they must resubmit an application and start anew.

In 2003, the Best Managed program introduced a new category of winners, the Platinum Club. This elite level is open to companies that have been winners for at least six consecutive years, and they must apply for this designation.

To learn more about the Canada's 50 Best Managed Companies program, including how to apply for consideration as a winner, visit the program's website, www.canadas50best.com.

Foreword

According to legend, Alexander the Great, upon entering the city of Telmissus in ancient Phrygia, found there an ox cart tethered to a column of the temple to Zeus. The formidable knot securing the ox cart had been tied by Gordias, the Phrygian king. Oracles prophesied that whoever could untie this "Gordian knot" would be ruler of all Asia. Many had attempted to loosen the tangled mass, but it held fast.

Alexander never even broke a nail: he simply drew his sword and cut it. Zeus, admiring Alexander's initiative and unorthodox approach, honoured the prophesy, resulting in an immortality of deed for Alexander that few have equalled.

When it comes to understanding the sources of success in business, however, we hope in vain for an analogous solution. There is no magic bullet, no cure-all, no panacea, no Alexandrian sword to short-cut our quest. Our only hope lies in the patient unravelling of the complicated causes behind the success of the few and the failure of the many.

The perennially successful organizations profiled in these pages offer valuable insight into the evergreen issues that occupy, preoccupy, and all too often vex the management teams of companies of all sizes. From building actionable strategies, to financing, to focusing on customers, to leveraging technology, to leadership, the "what" of the lessons here holds few surprises. Instead, the payoff lies in the deeper insights their stories afford us into the specifics of "how" each company has solved these general problems in its own specific way.

It would be a mistake to seek within this anthology of triumph specific guidance for your own success; that would be tantamount to hoping that someone else can cut your personal Gordian knot. Your solutions will necessarily be different from those discovered or created by the exemplars offered here. The objective of this book is more modest: that you will find here valuable counsel and direction in your own never-ending search for answers to these same questions. And so my recommendation is to see each vignette not as the source of prescriptive advice but as an opportunity for the experiences of others to contribute to your own efforts to work free any one of the threads that binds you.

For in the end, even if cutting the Gordian knot is a powerful metaphor for Alexander's penchant for bold action, the laborious and painstaking untying of it would have been an appropriate metaphor for the unwavering dedication, commitment, and situation-specific insights it took to actually conquer Asia.

—Michael Raynor

Introduction

When we set out to create a book based on the Canada's 50 Best Managed Companies program, we were embracing an exceptional opportunity to provide management lessons from a remarkably diverse group of Canadian corporate success stories. In telling the stories of individual companies (and their top executives), we wanted to illustrate with each chapter, in an engaging case-study style, one of the ten criteria for management excellence found within the program's assessments of *strategy, capability,* and *commitment,* and to invite commentary from professionals at Deloitte and Queen's School of Business, partners in the Best Managed program. Management theory, after all, is only theory until you see it in actual practice.

The goal was not to provide a shopping list of companies in any given program year, or to prioritize companies that had appeared the greatest number of times. We were striving for diversity in industries (new economy and old, manufacturing and service), regions (from coast to coast), stages of development (a few years old to many decades), ownership (partially public and private, employee-owned, family-controlled), and annual revenues (in the companies we chose, from the tens of millions to the billions).

The awards program, which has been recognizing exceptional Canadian companies since 1993, provided a rich base of enterprises from which to choose, so much so that the challenge proved to lie in deciding which company best exemplified which criterion. Successful companies need to do many things well, not just any one thing. It's impossible for a company to successfully meet challenges associated with growth, for example, if it cannot also manage its finances or service its customers. Companies that make the Best Managed rankings must measure up to a broad range of diagnostics, and it's almost impossible for one to slip through that has significant flaws in some aspect of its performance.

Which all goes to say that there is not a company profiled in a particular chapter that could not have been the focus of one of the other chapters. National Leasing of Winnipeg was a natural choice for Chapter 10 (attracting and retaining talent to build an exceptional culture), but it could as easily have served in Chapter 9 (creating the right leadership and communicating the vision). Conversely, our subject for Chapter 9, Cirque du Soleil, would also have served capably in Chapter 10. Armour Transportation Systems, a good fit for Chapter 6 (developing and leveraging core competencies) could also ably have appeared in Chapter 2 (pursuing and managing alliances, acquisitions, and other strategic relationships) or Chapter 5 (building and sustaining a customer-focused approach to sales and marketing). The possible switches and substitutions are endless.

Nevertheless, we are confident that the company chosen for each chapter best illustrates the principle being explored, without meaning to imply that it excels at a principle above and beyond any other profiled company, or that a particular principle is necessarily its greatest (or only) strength. And as the reader explores the various chapters, certain common themes and shared experiences indeed will emerge. These go beyond small coincidences—such as the fact that it takes about the same number of people (around sixty) to staff a Boston Pizza restaurant as it does to perform a Cirque du Soleil show.

These successful companies, regardless of which chapter they have been chosen to anchor, place a high priority on understanding their customer base and servicing it to the utmost. They also are agile, flexible, able to change directions and strategies in a way that remains true to their core competencies. They understand who they are and what they do, but they are not rigid or blind to change and opportunity.

Successful companies understand their product, which might be a surprising statement, as it implies that many companies do not. But it is true that many, many businesses do not have a solid, strategic definition of the business they are in, of exactly what it is they are producing or providing. The reader will hear in these chapters executives emphasize the precise nature of their business in ways that their own industries might not recognize. Sometimes these definitions of "what we do" have been in the blood of the enterprise since the beginning. But often, they have emerged in response to internal or external challenges. Ownership and management had to step back, assess their own operations, the preconceived notions of their corporate culture, and the needs of the marketplace, and come up with a fresh understanding of their purpose and goals so that they could move forward profitably and with a better understanding of where opportunities lie and how the customer could be best satisfied.

Geoff Smith of EllisDon speaks to the "huge cultural change" his general contracting business was being put through at the time it was developing the software tool that is at the heart of the Chapter 4 case study. "We were changing EllisDon from viewing itself as a construction company to being a service company," Smith explains. "People got into the business because they like to build. But we're not builders. We're in a service industry that builds. We don't actually build a lot ourselves—the subcontractors do."

Over at Harry Rosen, Chapter 5, Larry Rosen explains how his upmarket men's clothing chain is "in the business of assisting men in developing a confident personal image, in all aspects of their life, any time, place, or occasion.... We don't perceive ourselves as being in the clothing business. We don't just sell suits and sport jackets. It's a relationship-based business."

And at Armour Transportation Systems, Chapter 6, Wesley Armour recalls his reaction to the jarring impact of deregulation on his trucking company: "When business became cutthroat, I said to my managers, 'What is our future here?' I decided that we had to be more than a trucker. We had to be a total supplier of transportation." His company stopped thinking of itself in terms of vehicles and drivers but, instead, in terms of what the customer needed and how Armour had to change and grow in order to provide it better than any competitor.

These individual chapters also tell stories: engaging ones, in which company founders and senior executives address frankly the challenges they have faced. One cannot listen to Rossana Di Zio Magnotta tell the story in Chapter 1 of the traumatic beginnings of the winery she founded with her husband, Gabe, and not appreciate viscerally the hurdles entrepreneurs who risk all on a dream often encounter. And because most of the profiled companies are held privately, the views afforded of their operations in this book are often an unprecedented glimpse of business practices and experiences that never appear in the media. For most business managers, the peek this book provides inside the workings of a private company—including the accounts of a company's travails long before it went public—provide a perspective on business practices rarely attainable otherwise, and which also closely align with their own circumstances.

As it will become clear to the reader, the individual industries in which these companies operate provide their own fascinating insights. Boston Pizza takes you into the restaurant franchise game, Spin Master into the world of Air Hogs and Shrinky Dinks. And Cirque du Soleil makes every senior manager want to run away to join the circus. But the larger lessons always come through. Chapter 8, exploring the PCL Construction Group of Companies, is not required reading solely for business people hoping to build airports and major museums. The company delivers a textbook study of how companies of any type and size need to design the right organizations and processes to support growth. And Chapter 7, on Mediagrif Interactive Technologies, is not of sole interest to e-commerce aficionados. Its achievements in attracting capital and managing finances speak directly to all entrepreneurs, regardless of their particular industry, who aspire to turn a vision into a business that can steer safely through the universal challenges of a start-up.

The lessons imparted in these chapters would not have been possible without the cooperation of the many owners and executives interviewed exclusively for this book. They were generous with their observations and experiences (and sometimes with their private financial data), knowing that their lessons would benefit others. They responded with unvarnished frankness to questions posed about setbacks or challenges. Their achievements give them considerable reason to be proud, but what is consistently impressive is a lack of boastfulness. This is in large part because senior executives well understand that the Best Managed program does not celebrate executives alone, that it is not some personal award of merit. The program recognizes *everyone* in a company. CEOs in turn recognize that their company's success is predicated on the innovation, commitment, and capabilities of their employees and management teams.

These are also people still fully engaged in meeting the challenges of business. They are not resting on laurels, and they are well aware that adversity is always lying in wait. Many speak to the difficulties of the last recession in the early 1990s, and everyone understands that the economic cycle is not yet dead. There will be rough spots in the road ahead for everyone. But what these companies have demonstrated consistently is an ability to roll with the punches, to turn seeming setbacks into opportunities. It's our hope that readers will be able to draw from these chapters lessons that make their own enterprises more competitive, more adaptable, more agile. And—as seems to be the case in so many of them—a more fun place to work and prosper.

The Deloitte perspective

For each chapter, the authors provide a concluding overview of its theme from the Deloitte perspective. The lessons provided by the particular company profile are presented in a concise format with actionable observations of benefit to enterprises large and small in all businesses and stages of growth. Deloitte professionals provide subject-specific guidance to expand on the chapter content with personal observations while applying company-specific insights to challenges faced by businesses in general.

Growth Insights, a global website operated by Deloitte Touche Tohmatsu, offers a diverse selection of materials related to the ten chapter themes gathered under the imperatives of strategy, capability, and commitment. It provides a comprehensive, research-backed view of the challenges facing today's growth companies. Growth Insights identifies the business issues that matter most to growth organizations, and showcases practical perspectives from both company executives and Deloitte practitioners on how to address these business issues. Visit the website at www.growth-insights.com.

Strategy

1 Ripe opportunities

Developing an executable strategy to achieve sustainable growth

Magnotta Winery

Canada's 50 Best Managed Companies winner, 2000–2004

Lest you doubt that Magnotta Winery's flagship operation in Vaughan is a major shopping destination for oenophiles, take note of the prominent roadside signage. Both northbound and southbound on Highway 400, signs guide drivers to the off-ramp that takes you westbound on Highway 7, just north of Toronto. Another sign deflects you north on Weston Road, and then another one, quickly right on Chrislea Road. The winery, which is also home to a brewery—and, soon, a fifteen-hundred-square-foot distillery—is right around the corner. But just before you turn onto Chrislea, having followed all that helpful roadside signage that Magnotta has paid the Ontario government to erect, you cannot help but notice a brand new LCBO outlet, one of over six hundred stores the Liquor Control Board of Ontario operates in the province.

Mention this LCBO outlet to Rossana Di Zio Magnotta, the winery's co-founder, and she smiles knowingly, even tolerantly—which is saying something, given the history between her family's business and the province's official alcohol retailing and regulating behemoth. "It followed us here," she says matter-of-factly. Indeed, it is as if the LCBO followed the same set of signs as Magnotta Winery's loyal customers: This way to spectacular retail sales. People who shop at the flagship Magnotta outlet, having driven past the LCBO store to reach it, probably spend twice as much per visit as a typical LCBO drive-by shopper. LCBO customers province-wide spend on average around $30 per visit, while Magnotta's customers are dropping around $60. And they're doing so for first-class product that sells for less than comparable offerings at the LCBO.

Rossana is able to say cheerful things about the Liquor Control Board of Ontario these days, even speaking of an "alliance" between it and her company. But it wasn't long ago that Magnotta and the LCBO were hardened adversaries in a decade-long legal struggle, before a mediated settlement was announced (no details were ever disclosed) in May 2001. Rossana and Gabe, her husband of more than thirty years, have made a tremendous success of a venture that nearly failed in its opening moments when the LCBO informed them there was no shelf space for their product. About fifteen years ago, they had mortgaged their house and risked everything to establish a winery. Repudiation forced Rossana and Gabe into a hurried offensive huddle to come up with an alternate business model before they were ruined. The new plan turned out so well that one would be forgiven for thinking it had been their intention from the start. But it wasn't. "The LCBO created the path we followed," Rossana says.

But before setting out on that path after the LCBO rejection, Rossana volunteers, she cried for two weeks. Then, as the saying goes, it was down to business. In a matter of months, Magnotta was one of the largest wineries in Ontario. Today, Magnotta is the province's third largest, with almost $30 million in sales in 2005, outranked only by giants Vincor and Andrés, which enjoyed a critical—and essentially insurmountable—jumpstart (as we shall see) in the regulatory oddities of provincial wine retailing, and between them account for an estimated 75 percent of the domestic wine industry in Canada.

Magnotta's stock is traded on the Toronto Stock Exchange (TSX), and while Gabe is chairman and CEO, it's Rossana, the president, who is most identified with the enterprise. She is its public face, and anything but a figurehead. She has had a huge impact on her industry, and it's safe to say that when the LCBO bureaucrats declined to allow her and her husband to sell their wines through the government outlets, they weren't fully aware of what Rossana Magnotta was capable of in response. Because, frankly, at that time, neither was she.

In 1954, an immigrant couple—one of them a cabinetmaker, the other a clothing designer—arrived in Canada from central Italy's Abruzzi region, eighteen-month-old Rossana in tow. The Di Zios were headed for The Porcupine, the northern Ontario mining district, with Timmins at its centre. Chief exports: gold from the Dome and McIntyre mines, and professional hockey players, including Frank Mahovlich, Bill Barilko, and Allan Stanley. The family moved into a house in Schumacher. Little Rossana's father went from job to job, a cabinetmaker adrift in a colony of hard-rock miners. Her mother sized up the figure skating going on at the McIntyre Arena in Schumacher. It was a sport she knew nothing about, except that costumes were required, and she launched a business designing and sewing them.

In 1959, the Di Zio family moved to Toronto. Rossana grew up to become a medical lab technologist and married Gabe, who had arrived in Canada from Italy at age eleven. Gabe launched a series of business ventures, trying to find one that clicked. Finally, there was success in 1985 with Festa Juice Co. Ltd. (now a wholly owned Magnotta subsidiary), which makes grape juice for the home wine market.

The province had just revised its regulations on homemade wine. It had always been legal to make your own wine and serve it to friends and family, provided it wasn't sold. The important change in the regulations was that for events in public spaces such as social clubs and banquet halls, which require a Special Occasion Permit to serve or sell alcohol, homemade wine now could also be served, again provided there was no charge for it. The new regulation delighted the ethnic communities in which home winemaking had a long-standing tradition but riled the wine industry, which relied on bulk sales for social events.

Once the children began arriving (there are three), Rossana stayed home to raise them, keeping up her medical technology qualifications through course work. But she became drawn into winemaking, fascinated by it. It was an adjunct of her fondness for cooking. She began making wine not only from Festa's juice but from "anything imaginable," including dandelions. Her husband, she explains, "had the business side, but not the technical side." Rossana's lab background gave her the means to delve into the chemistry of winemaking, the sugars and acid balances. She decided to give Gabe a hand in the juice business, providing expertise that customers were looking for, while still raising the kids. "I'm going to open up my own little laboratory and show people how to make wine," is how she describes her decision. Gabe and Rossana opened a store from which to sell Festa juice, and at which Rossana operated a lab that provided free analysis of their customers' wine.

There were cultural problems immediately, however. The Festa customer base was mainly in Toronto's Greek, Portuguese, and Italian communities, where overwhelmingly the men of the household make the wine. The craft was passed down from father to son, and much tradition and pride was bound up in the exercise. "Here I was, telling these guys how to make wine. Some were offended. I wrote a book, so they could follow the written instructions." It was called *Six Easy Steps to Making Wine the Festa Way*. Rossana had it translated into the languages of her customers, and gave it away with the purchase of Festa juice. Word got around about *La Signora* who could help you with your winemaking. She became the lady you went to if you wanted someone to "repair" your wine. The tight-knit communities that were Festa's main customer base made Rossana famous: If you could convince one Portuguese or Italian man that there was a better way to make his wine, he would tell his brothers, and his cousins. Festa's business selling grape juice grew with Rossana's celebrity.

"People began asking us for ready-made wine, but that would have been bootlegging," Rossana recalls. She and Gabe recognized the opportunity to go into the winemaking business as an offshoot of Festa. They had a ready customer base—the customers Rossana was advising at Festa who couldn't necessarily make enough wine for home and special occasions. All the Magnottas had to do was start a winery. And that brought them into the tangle of regulations controlling the Ontario wine industry.

The Liquor Control Board of Ontario didn't just serve as the main retailer of wine and spirits in the province. It also licensed production, determined pricing, and, until just a few years ago, vetted advertising. The easiest way to get that production licence was to buy an existing winery, which is what Gabe and Rossana did, acquiring the assets (but not the land) of a husband-and-wife shop called Charal in 1989 for $250,000. There was no vineyard, and the Magnottas didn't have all the necessary equipment. But the T.G. Bright operation in Niagara Falls was shutting down, and its stainless-steel tanks were available. (In 1993, Bright merged with Cartier Inniskillin Vintners to become Vincor International.) Gabe pulled off a half-mad purchase, buying more tanks than they could afford or use—some of them never would have fit in the building they were leasing for the new winery—and counting on being able to flip some of them immediately so that the cheque he wrote to pay for them all wouldn't bounce. "He wrote a cheque that didn't exist," is how Rossana puts it. "But if we had waited another day, we would have missed the boat."

They moved the equipment into an industrial space in Concord, in what is now the city of Vaughan. To sell their wine, they naturally turned to the province's sanctioned retailer, the LCBO. And that's when the shock came. Rossana says they were in discussions with the LCBO about it carrying four Magnotta varietals. Then the LCBO flat out refused to give them any shelf space. They were told to come back in a year and try again.

It was a devastating setback. The Magnottas had assumed that they would sell their wine through the LCBO. They hadn't considered the possibility that the LCBO might decide not to sell their wine. The rejection by the liquor board came atop a steep recession. There hadn't been a Plan B, and the alternatives to selling through the LCBO were extremely limited. An Ontario winery is permitted to sell its product at the point of production, and while this avenue was open to Magnotta, Gabe and Rossana hadn't chosen their winery site with consumer appeal in mind. No thought had been given to its location in terms of their consumer base. And it was in an uninspiring industrial setting, not on a charming estate on the Niagara Peninsula, the province's main viticulture area.

The province's estate wineries were beginning to gain momentum around the time the Magnottas decided to enter the business, and this may have been a factor in the LCBO's refusal to stock Magnotta's wine. Both the LCBO and the Ontario wine industry had an image problem: Ontario wine had a long-standing reputation for being, well, cheap plonk, and the LCBO had a reputation, even as quality Ontario estate wineries began to emerge, for favouring foreign rather than domestic producers in its retailing. Both sides were striving to address this problem through the creation of a new marketing vehicle, the Vintners Quality Alliance, or VQA. Only varietal wines made from Ontario-grown grapes would qualify for the VQA seal of approval. (While this was a volunteer system when introduced, the Vintners Quality Alliance Act of 1999, which became law in June 2000, set specific legal guidelines for wines carrying the VQA imprimatur.) Along came Magnotta, a new venture in an industrial setting making wine from Festa juice, just as the LCBO was committing marketing resources to the VQA initiative.

Not everything being produced by Ontario wineries, of course, was or is VQA. Wines can be made from juice from domestic or international producers. And "blending," the mixing of domestic wine with offshore wines to produce low-cost table wines, is also permitted, provided that at least 30 percent of the content is made from Ontario grapes; otherwise the product is considered an import.

And Magnotta had another competitive disadvantage, which it was not able to overcome. The LCBO had issued licences for off-premises retail operations to a number of Ontario wineries, a practice it stopped in 1987 as a result of the free trade agreement between Canada and the United States. Having come along two years too late, Magnotta couldn't get a licence to open a kiosk in a shopping mall, for example, while its largest competitors could, and had. As the industry consolidated in the 1990s, the two leading players, Andrés and Vincor, would come to operate between them more than 260 of the province's 290 off-premises retail sites through their respective Vineyards Estate Wines and WineRack outlets. These off-premises retail operations, known to many consumers through small stand-alone kiosks or stores in a shopping mall, often just beyond the checkout counters of a supermarket, accounted for 36 percent of all Ontario wine sales in 2004.

And Magnotta, it must be said, had to contend with the dark cloud cast over its treasured Festa clientele by allegations of bootlegging in the ethnic communities. The province's wine industry was deeply exercised about alleged illegal sales by home-based winemakers. At a 1991 session of the provincial government's Standing Committee on General Government, a deputation by the Wine Council of Ontario, meeting to address the issue of cross-border shopping, veered into a tirade against Magnotta's customer base (neither Magnotta nor Festa were specifically named). In response to a question from one committee member, the council's spokesperson intoned: "The large-scale production of homemade wine for regular use by families in their own houses is indeed, to a great extent, found among specific ethnic groups—the Portuguese, the Italians, and many others. The development of what I call the commercial home winemaking business—that is, wine produced by unlicensed people and sold—appears to have started in the southwestern part of Ontario, between Hamilton and Windsor-Sarnia, but I believe it has spread fairly widely and fairly significantly since the rules were changed to permit the use of homemade wine legally."

No one was accusing Magnotta or Festa of being in the bootlegging business, but the success of Festa in supplying juice to the home-based winemakers—and Rossana's helpful winemaking guide—probably didn't smooth Magnotta Winery's entry into the ranks of Ontario's commercial wineries. Yet, ironically, the Magnottas had gone to the expense of establishing a legitimate winery precisely because they wouldn't consider selling wine illegally through Festa Juice.

"I watched my parents struggle, trying to do so well for their family," Rossana recalls. "My father would say, 'I'd rather live on bread and water than do something unethical.' I still have flashbacks, of my mother making clothes for me out of my father's old shirts. The clothes were beautiful, but still ... Today, we don't take anything for granted. And we fight for what we believe in, for what is right."

From the beginning, Magnotta was an outsider in the Ontario wine trade, thanks to the LCBO's refusal to stock the start-up's product. When the LCBO rejected Magnotta, "We had an emergency marketing meeting," says Rossana. It consisted of a husband and wife staring into a deep financial hole, in which they had deposited their personal assets. The burning question was, what are we going to do, dear?

"I was shaking to death when we had to mortgage the house," says Rossana. "But once I was thrown into the arena, I found out how much of a fighter I am. I never thought I had an entrepreneurial bone in my body. I thought I was a technical person doing morphology, working behind the scenes to help the pathologist. I never thought I'd be a 'front' person, and take risks. But I learned you could take calculated risks. Those are okay. And the vision has always been there."

With no other options available, the Magnottas realized they would have to sell their wine directly to the public, as their winery licence permitted. They already had experience with the Festa store, but it was not what they had had in mind for the winery. But desperation shaped their new business plan, and the winery store opened in December 1990. It proved to be an almost overnight success.

"One of the things about Magnotta that is really striking is the outright managerial commitment," says Ken Wong, associate professor of business and marketing strategy at Queen's School of Business. "It's one thing to talk about change and say, 'We're committed to growth.' It's another thing to put your heart and soul into it. Magnotta is a classic entrepreneurial story of 'never say die.' Another thing that impresses me is how they were hit with an external change and dealt with it. Many companies come up with a stop-gap measure. But with Magnotta, they really thought it through." The company and the business plan, Wong notes, changed to confront the reality. Magnotta didn't just sell temporarily for a year or two while it tried to get in the door of the LCBO: The winery was reconceived around the concept of it doing its own retailing.

"We never thought in a million years we'd grow so quickly," Rossana says. Within a few months of the store opening, Magnotta was the fifth largest winery by sales volume in Ontario. It wasn't selling through the LCBO—in fact, it was suing the LCBO. The Wine Council of Ontario was lobbying to make it illegal to serve homemade wine at public functions.

The campaign against homemade wine was verging on shrill, and at times was offensive. One wine importer charged that "the illegal market is largely due to a large population of Italians in Ontario, some of whom illegally sell these wines to restaurants out of 'wineries' established in their homes to avoid the high tax." The Canadian Wine Institute, the industry's national lobby group, released a report in 1994 that made astonishing claims about the size of the illegal wine market. It charged that more than one-third of all wine purchased in Canada was illegally produced, and that for every ten bottles of table wine sold in Ontario through the LCBO and winery stores, another twelve came from sources unaccounted for.

And apparently, homemade wine was also all but killing people. Allegations were made about deadly levels of cyanide and other harmful impurities being discovered in homemade product (though no deaths were ever reported). The LCBO meanwhile defended its monopoly by citing the revenue it was pumping into provincial social programs—a public relations practice it continues. It didn't take much imagination for the average consumer to conclude that wine not sold through a government store was taking food from the mouths of the underprivileged, and that bootleg wine made from legitimately retailed grape juice was a monstrous health risk and threatened the survival of the domestic wine industry.

In the midst of this hysteria, Magnotta was building its sales volume and market share by creating a business plan that not only confronted the regulatory restrictions imposed on it but turned them to its advantage.

An eye-opener for the Magnottas had been just how much markup there was on wine sold at the LCBO. They had already gone through the pricing process when they learned the LCBO wouldn't stock their product. LCBO reserves the right to set pricing, including minimum pricing. One of its justifications was (and still is) equalization, ensuring that high-volume, low-cost foreign producers, particularly of table wines, or *vin ordinaire,* didn't significantly underprice domestic production. At the same time that the Wine Council of Ontario was alleging massive bootlegging in the home wine industry, it was also complaining to the province about the degree of markup imposed by the LCBO, which it said was causing consumers in border areas to dash into the United States to buy wine at significant savings.

The pricing system used by the LCBO is complex, but Rossana says the markup it was proposing for Magnotta's wine gave the province a 58 percent profit margin. The Magnottas would also be charged an additional $1.62 per litre for warehousing and distribution. "We asked ourselves, where are we going to make money? We figured wineries must be losing their shirts on table wines."

Now that they weren't welcome at the LCBO, the Magnottas were free to come up with their own pricing for the sales at a winery store. "We realized our wine had to have a much lower cost than at the LCBO, to get people to come out to the store. We decided to sell our wine for $3.95. We'd have to sell it for double that at the LCBO, and we'd make less than we would on our own."

And that is how Magnotta got off the ground. Confronted with a retailing crisis, squeezed by a fierce recession, the winery was compelled to adopt a "cheap wine" strategy at its own winery store. The media caught wind of the start-up, and started paying visits to the winery. Rossana gives special credit to CBC Radio host Joe Coté for helping the winery break through with a sceptical public, declaring that the wine might be priced at $3.95, "but it's good." Print media such as the *Toronto Star* and *The Globe and Mail* also gave it positive coverage. The "but it's good" message began to spread. Word of mouth drove sales upward. "We grew fivefold in five months. We sold at an unheard-of price, but we did not give them an inferior product," says Rossana.

Many of the winery's first customers came from the ranks of the Festa customers, the contacts Rossana had made in the home wine community. Price was a major motivator, but as Rossana acknowledges, "there was an antigovernment streak in many of the early customers. It was, 'Let's support these folks because they're working hard.'"

Locked in litigation with the LCBO, Magnotta continued with its direct sales, and continued to grow. Dependent on its own retailing, Magnotta could expand only by buying small Ontario wineries (including their licences) and strategically relocating them in southern Ontario, where retail sales were strongest. The Magnottas came to own five wineries this way, and in the process acquired store licences that allowed them to open two retail outlets without wineries attached to them.

As sales grew, the Magnottas realized that, irrespective of their success, they were developing a brand image problem. They were known as the "cheap wine" company. They would try to explain to new customers the pricing structure of the LCBO, why their wine was at least as good as a bottle costing twice as much at the government outlet. "Some listened," says Rossana, "but most people didn't care." The wine was good, and it was cheap. End of story. But Magnotta was having a terrible time attracting wine aficionados—not only de facto wine snobs but connoisseurs, as well as casual drinkers who associate price in wines with quality and status. For them, inexpensive wine, especially inexpensive Ontario wine, signified plonk. The status-conscious couldn't impress guests by putting a bottle of Magnotta on the dinner table.

Magnotta was facing a classic marketing dilemma. Studies were telling it that in a high-quality product sector, consumers have a hard time accepting a low cost. Cheaper simply must mean inferior. If an auto manufacturer brought out a car that was supposed to be as good as or better than a Mercedes-Benz but was priced like a Hyundai, the consumer was wont to be sceptical about its quality.

Perhaps surprisingly, Magnotta did not seize upon the solution of giving a lot of people what they appeared implicitly to want: a higher price. If consumers didn't understand the LCBO pricing system, they wouldn't understand why Magnotta could sell direct from the winery at such a low price and still maintain a decent profit margin. (Its gross profit margin in 2004 was 49 percent.) So why not simply charge a price these consumers were prepared to accept, and reap scandalous profit margins?

That option was a non-starter. The low price was a reward for customers going out of their way to come to the winery to spend their money, rather than shopping at the neighbourhood LCBO or at a retail outlet near the supermarket checkout. Magnotta wasn't looking for higher margins than it deserved.

"You need to sell things at a profit and pay your bills," says Rossana. "But if you want long-term growth, you can't be greedy." And from the beginning, the winery generated considerable customer loyalty. "It's dog eat dog," Rossana says of the wine business. "You have to find your niche. Our customer appreciation is real and comes from the top down. We have built a unique interest and respect from the consumer. We worked very hard and earned every penny we made. Some of the best customers have been with us through the struggles. We're a people's company, and people like that."

"Despite all the external shocks," Wong notes, "what hasn't changed is Magnotta's single-minded focus on the customer. It's been an important part of its sustainability."

And Magnotta has always been price conscious. "Price," says marketing manager Cynthia Young, "is part of our brand." When a Magnotta product wins a competition award—and there have been over twenty-three hundred of them—the price does not change. A Chardonnay that won gold at a competition in France continued to sell at $16.95 to the very last bottle.

---

* SOLUTION

As it happened, it was competitions that Magnotta turned to as the means to hammer home the "affordable excellence" tag line that Gabe and Rossana had long given to their wines. Ironically, their success in competitions also led them to abandon the tag line. In 2001, they secured the aid of a branding company to deal with the Magnotta conundrum. Sales had reached a plateau. They were simply unable to break through with what Rosanna calls the "Audi crowd." The branding exercise caused them to abandon any mention of affordability and shift over to the simple tag line "The Award Winning Winery."

"Awards became the main focus," says Young, who came aboard at the time of the 2001 branding exercise. "Now we have to continually win awards. Once we say it, we can't move back." But Magnotta has also embraced the awards process as part of its quality-control regimen. Magnotta always enters in competition the same wines that can be purchased on its retail shelves, rather than special batches. If a particular wine continually wins bronzes or honourable mentions, that's a sign for Magnotta to have a hard look at how it's producing that wine, and how it might be improved.

Magnotta had come to see its future in premium wines, those products with higher price points and that invite accolades at competition. "We didn't want to be the table wine company," says

Rossana. Magnotta has invested in its own vineyards: four totalling 180 acres in the Niagara Peninsula, in the 1990s, and a further 351 acres in Chile's Maipo Valley, in 1996. As of 2005, Magnotta's vineyards provided 31 percent of its wine and grape requirements. Many of Magnotta's premium reds come from its own vineyards. "If you want to be in premium wines," Rossana explains, "you have to have a way of controlling the grape, right from the earth." The breadth of the company's excellence is reflected in Magnotta's being the first and only Canadian winery to have won four Black Diamond awards for consistency and quality at the InterVin international wine competition, rewarded for having the most gold medals in a competition.

The strategy of moving upmarket, along with a marketing shift that placed an emphasis on lifestyle rather than price point, paid off. In the under-$10 table wine category, Magnotta has maintained its historic sales. But it has increased revenues in the $10 to $15 range by $400,000, and the $15 to $20 range by $300,000. Over the last three fiscal years, increases in net earnings outstripped net sales 17.4 to 5.2 percent.

"When Magnotta went to the premium brands," says Wong, "there had to be a different way of communicating quality." It didn't try to take its existing line of wines and price it up, making them something they weren't. It developed award-winning products that earned their own following. And, says Wong, "the company had the good sense to keep in mind what it is known for, and that is affordability. It was happy being an Acura, not a Rolls-Royce. It built on the strength of its relationship with customers, on its affordability, and I think gained some snob appeal." Wong can well imagine certain customers who know their wine, but also delight in serving a great wine that they can tell friends only cost them "eighteen bucks instead of thirty or forty."

"We made an Amarone-style VQA wine," Rossana offers, as an example of Magnotta's move upmarket. "My husband had wanted to do it. It was his dream to prove to the world we could make the top reds in Ontario." Called Enotrium, it was a first for the Ontario wine industry. "We invested in the facility, and released the first vintage last year [2004]. Sixteen hundred bottles sold out in three months. People wanted to hear the story of how we did it, and came in to listen."

Over time, this story of Magnotta's various adventures has proved to be a major attraction for consumers. They like to come into the stores, hear about how the company started, about how a particular varietal or specialty product like ice grappa came about or is made. They can see the winery, join a tour if they wish. Magnotta has entire neighbourhoods show up. "Other wineries treat wine as a commodity," says Young. "It's something people buy at the end of a visit to the grocery store. We've found that it's the experience of wine that people are seeking. The tasting, the talking." The things they can't experience from a dash in and out of an LCBO or while pushing a shopping cart past a mall kiosk.

Magnotta has made wine purchasing an exercise in conversation, and in learning. Consumers find out what cheese goes best with what wine. They ask why Magnotta decided to make a sparkling ice wine. They go home with the ice wine story and share it with friends as they serve it. Magnotta has also made a strong connection not only between wine and food but with art: The design of the bottle labels was based on original artworks the Magnottas had hanging on the walls of their home. Today, the company has an extensive corporate art collection. The works that appear on labels are also on display.

Having been forced by the LCBO to resort to winery store sales, Magnotta has made its stores a focal point of the business. "To survive," says Rossana, "we had to be a one-stop shopping experience." The flagship store in Vaughan recently underwent a major aesthetic overhaul, and the other stores are undergoing the same; in April 2005 the Brampton location was moved to a new site, expanding from 2000 to 5600 square feet, mainly to increase the retail space so that the company's product line could be better showcased. Magnotta has also expanded beyond wines, entering the brewing business in the mid-1990s, and in 2005 was in the process of completing a 1500-square-foot addition to the Vaughan operation for an onsite distillery. Vaughan would soon have a winery, a premium brewery, and a distillery all under one roof.

Magnotta's stores offer not only its wine but also wine- and beer-making products, glassware, and other finery associated with wining and dining. The company also sought alliances, co-hosting showcasing and tasting events with producers of foods such as cheese that made for natural pairings. It struck up a partnership with Humber College's hospitality and tourism program; some exams actually take place at Magnotta. It also opened an eighth "store," a website, through which it can ship orders by Canada Post to customers. "We're making some people in Northern Ontario very happy," Rossana notes. They still have one man who drives to Magnotta from Florida every year, just to shop in person.

And, the battle with the LCBO having ended with the mediated settlement of 2001, Magnotta product can now be found in Vintages, the LCBO's upmarket outlets. "Everything's fine now," says Rossana. "We have a great relationship with the liquor board. I have to be honest. We haven't had any problems." It's helped that Magnotta no longer has to submit its advertising for approval to the LCBO, which was—and remains to a substantial degree—a direct retail competitor, since that vetting responsibility has been transferred to the province's Alcohol and Gaming Commission.

Magnotta sells its premium ice wines through Vintages. "But we could pull out and be fine," Rossana says. Selling through Vintages, however, is "a gesture of goodwill on both our parts. The lawsuit was a volatile period, and it put a lot of strain on the company. On the way, we did a lot to change the industry." Indeed, the major wineries have stopped fighting the homemade trade and have added subsidiaries to supply the do-it-yourself market.

"Being in the LCBO," Rossana adds, "helps us brand." In September 2004, Magnotta was Vintage's winery of the month. Magnotta placed six limited-edition wines with the government retailer. "The consumer got a tease," Rossana Di Zio Magnotta says, then adds with a smile, "They had to come to Magnotta to get more."

The Deloitte perspective

Developing an executable strategy to achieve sustainable growth

A founder's vision for his or her company usually doesn't change. It's the strategy and tactics to achieve that vision that are constantly in motion. The Magnotta strategy was one that was certainly not clear when Gabe and Rosanna started the business. Their aim was to produce quality wine and sell it to consumers through the standard retail channel, the Liquor Control Board of Ontario. But when the LCBO declined to stock their product, they had to find a different way to achieve the vision of being a quality wine producer. They rapidly developed strategic options using a creative process that relied heavily on their assessment of their external environment, while matching the capabilities of their organization to address those key issues. There had never been a plan to be the dominant player in the wine industry, but the strategic options they chose nevertheless permitted them to become the third-largest winery in the province.

One of Magnotta's strategies was to grow sales through brand evolution and innovation. Its ice wine and Amarone-style VQA wine are prime examples of its ability to deliver on that promise. Innovation also steadily evolved from the reality the Magnottas confronted at the founding of their company: that they would have to be their own retailer. That led Magnotta Winery to focus relentlessly on the customer and defining its product in part by the purchase experience.

The one word that captures the strategic planning process for Magnotta is "alignment." When you consider the company's history and its position in the Ontario wine industry today, it has demonstrated an ability to align its vision, strategies, people, competencies, infrastructure, and technology all toward a single goal of producing an exceptional customer experience with its wine.

Strategies for today's companies, including ones like Magnotta, are not linear. CEOs need to appreciate that:

- Strategies evolve over time.
- Certain strategies need to be abandoned and new ones developed while gathering new internal and external information.
- The process of strategy formulation and execution cannot be done independently and are often done simultaneously.
- The entire organization, its network, and stakeholders should be leveraged to drive new strategic ideas.

2 Learning to play with others

Pursuing and managing alliances, acquisitions, and other strategic relationships

Spin Master

Canada's 50 Best Managed Companies winner, 2000–2004

"A color-change laminate comprising a substrate and formed thereon a porous layer which comprises a low-refractive-index pigment dispersed in a binder resin and tenaciously adherent thereto is disclosed. The porous layer becomes transparent or translucent upon absorption of a liquid medium, e.g., water to give a variety of visual changes. The low-refractive-index pigment contains at least a finely particulate silicic acid produced by the wet process...."

So reads the abstract of U.S. Patent no. 6,416,853, issued July 9, 2002. A secret formula for military camouflage, perhaps? No—it's the ingenious basis of a children's toy, called AquaDoodle, a white mat about three feet square that comes with a special pen filled with tap water. When a child draws on the mat with the refillable pen, the white fabric turns blue (that is, "the porous layer becomes transparent or translucent upon absorption of a liquid medium"). The mat is dry to the touch after being drawn on. There's no mess—a life-altering revelation to parents who have seen what children can do to drywall and upholstery with felt markers—and in a few minutes, when the water evaporates, the mat turns white again, ready for more doodling. Little wonder *Parenting* magazine gave an approving profile in October 2004 to this new offering from Spin Master Ltd. of Toronto.

Spin Master did not invent AquaDoodle. The patent belongs to The Pilot Ink Co., Ltd. of Japan. Pilot's products in turn are represented in North America by Funanuf of Los Angeles, which brought the concept to Spin Master's attention. Nor does Spin Master make AquaDoodle—at least not in a traditional industrial sense, in a factory of its own. The patented mat surface is made in Japan, and the finished product is stitched together in China.

So what is it, exactly, that Spin Master does? Just about everything you could ask of an innovative children's products company.

"A lot of our global alliances are predicated on the reputation of the company," says Ronnen Harary, one of Spin Master's three co-founders, who serves as co-CEO. His fellow co-founders are Anton Rabie (president and co-CEO) and Ben Varadi (executive vice-president). "We're known for our strength in sales, product performance, and quality marketing. We'll get the awareness of a product out."

"I think Spin Master is a unique group of people," says Dave Fuhrer, head of Funanuf. "It starts right at the top with those three guys, who have created a real entrepreneurial energy. There's a dramatic difference between it and Mattel or Hasbro, which are much more conventional companies." Fuhrer does business with both industry giants, and has good relations with them as well, but before a product is brought to market by them, it will endure an ordeal-by-fire of focus groups and screening from the advertising side of the business.

"Spin Master guys are reacting from the gut," Fuhrer notes. "They say: 'That's a great product. Let's figure out how we're going to do it.'" They manage to avoid what Fuhrer says is "the paralysis-through-analysis cliché. They roll up their sleeves and ask, how to we make this happen? They'll do it, even if it doesn't fit a product category of the company. There's a culture of, how do we do this?, not, why we can't do this? It's really refreshing."

Ken Wong, associate professor of business and marketing strategy at Queen's School of Business, cites the ability of the company's principals to trust their instincts and listen to all available input, rather than relying on formal market studies and focus-group tests, for creating their track record of successes. "I could picture one of them at a family get-together and some aunt corners him and starts to talk to him about what's wrong with toys. At any other company, the aunt would be given polite air time. But these guys would discuss and listen and take it all away with them. That's their market research. They really do listen to suppliers and everyone else. Their challenge is going to be staying in touch with the kids market as they grow older themselves. But while there's a certain risk to their method, it's a calculated risk."

Spin Master was founded in 1994 on a hare-brained idea, struck upon by the three friends from the University of Western Ontario: Ronnen Harary, who earned an honours bachelor's degree in political science, and Anton Rabie and Ben Varadi, who both graduated with an honours bachelor's degree from the Richard Ivey School of Business. Their idea? A model pantyhose-covered head that sprouted grass "hair" when watered. Ten thousand dollars in (pardon the pun) seed money later, Earth Buddy was born.

Spin Master today compares Earth Buddy to the Pet Rock, which is being a little unfair to itself—at least Earth Buddy *did* something. It was more like a Chia Pet for the organically amused. From a big-picture perspective, what this low-tech novelty did was launch Spin Master, one of the most interesting and successful child-products companies around.

It may be an axiom of free enterprise that the businesses that look as though they should be the most fun are actually among the toughest in which to succeed. While it's difficult to think of something that ought to be more fun than creating toys for children, the toy business is also one of the most nail-biting sectors of the Western economy. Making kids happy in a consistently profitable way is a hard nut to crack. But Spin Master has found a way to do it, not only by *not* being a toy company in the purest sense, but by not being a company at all, in the traditional sense.

Earth Buddy was an inauspicious start, yet today, Spin Master is a company with an increasing international presence. It is a first-class example of how an enterprise can grow and prosper, and remain agile and responsive, by building alliances rather than brick-and-mortar operations. Spin Master has sought strategic relationships with a broad spectrum of industry players, from inventors to toy brokers to international distributors to manufacturers to retailers to brand licensors. Just like a good kid's play activity, Spin Master teaches you how to excel by getting along well with others.

No company can achieve sustainable growth on its own. Success depends on productive alliances, which exist even if management isn't thinking of them strictly in those terms. Precious few enterprises are self-contained operations. Manufacturers require raw materials; products usually reach the marketplace through retailers and distributors. Sometimes such elements of the business process are owned by the enterprise, but often they're not.

Over time, North American enterprises, greatly influenced by Japanese business models, have come to see relationships with third parties from a new perspective. Where there might have been an adversarial relationship—suppliers being pushed for the lowest cost and not considered to be a strategic partner, trade unions and workforces locking horns with owners on bottom-dollar issues rather than considering their mutual well-being—management began to forge alliances. In manufacturing, this was abetted by the outsourcing of component fabrication, especially as the auto industry stopped trying to build automobiles entirely in-house. In many enterprises, it began to make financial sense to get out of manufacturing altogether, contracting production to domestic and offshore businesses. In some cases, product development, in R&D and design, began to move in whole or in part to independent firms and studios.

This trend was part and parcel of many companies recognizing their core competencies, focusing their internal energies, human capital, and investment dollars on the aspects of their business at which they excelled, reducing their overhead costs during start-up and early-stage growth, and avoiding credit-draining capital expenditures and staffing burdens. It became a given that if you were establishing a software company, you didn't need a factory to produce the CDs, and to avoid a ruinous burn rate in investment capital, you were better off outsourcing some of your traditional corporate functions.

At the same time, savvy companies have recognized that there is more to successful sustainable growth than adhering to a lean, competency-focused enterprise structure. To grow the top line, new markets have to be conquered, and market share increased.

These goals cannot necessarily be—nor ought they be—achieved alone. The cooperation of other ventures is both required and desired. In some cases, outright acquisition of an existing company in a new market to gain its products, its local knowledge, and its intellectual capital makes far more sense than striving to establish a beachhead and engaging in years of costly competition. In other cases, formal alliances, or new ventures in which equity is shared, make sense.

Alliances also involve looking beyond the enterprise's particular business sector for beneficial synergies. Products that are produced at or close to the level of commodities, with little differentiation in design and quality from competing items, benefit enormously from branding alliances. One children's lunchbox is pretty much the same as another—until one has the face of Spider-Man on it and the other doesn't. But producers of innovative products, with market recognition of their own, can team up through alliances that produce net gains for all parties, either in the nature of the end product, or the manner in which sales are promoted or achieved. A recent textbook example of powerful cross-pollination of brands occurred when BMW and Apple Inc. joined forces to create the first iPod-ready automobiles. Beginning with the 2002 model year, BMW offered models with iPod connectivity and song selection through controls embedded in the steering wheel. Selling more iPods and more BMWs wasn't as important as seizing an opportunity to enhance the cool factor of two well-recognized global consumer brands.

Alliances also bring together parties with relative strengths whose cooperation produces results that neither could achieve on their own. A typical example is an enterprise with strength in sales and marketing making the connection with one that knows how to create great products but not how to sell them. As generalists, neither would be particularly successful. But as specialists, they maximize the value they bring to discrete parts of the creation of a product or service—from concept through development, production, and delivery—and by partnering with other specialists, realize a success that would otherwise elude everyone.

This is by no means a case of individual companies simply addressing operational weaknesses. Rather, it's a case of companies being able to focus on what they do best, and not being burdened by business activities into which they need not expand. The alliance allows each party to remain flexible and dynamic, and to avoid numerous pitfalls in management. Companies that have a traditional sprawl of operations and divisions can struggle to find senior executives and board members who understand all aspects of the enterprise—and when they do find a generalist to serve as a leader, they can lose the spark of inspiration that is critical to the core business activity. Conversely, a company led by someone who has an admirable grasp of the core business can founder because this leader cannot make the managerial leap required to oversee diverse operations and the layers of executives that go along with them.

Every company that begins as an idea in somebody's garage must come to grips with some degree of operational expansion as its sales grow. But successful growth often depends on knowing how far to grow, and in which direction. Linear growth in revenues and market share do not require a matching geometric growth in corporate complexity.

Spin Master has worked assiduously with a business model that upholds the value of alliances in all aspects of its operations, and has been rewarded with growth and accolades in an industry that lately has left plenty of participants reeling.

The toy business is worth more than $20 billion retail in the United States alone (and the industry is overwhelmingly measured by the U.S. market), but that's a value the market has been struggling to maintain. The traditional toy market (which excludes the upstart video and computer games) has been flatlining for about a decade. U.S. sales were $19.1 billion in 1996, according to industry analyst the NPD Group, and after reaching $23 billion in 1999 and 2000, figures were in retreat. While NPD found some reasons to be hopeful in the "minimal" 3 percent decline in sales (by its estimate) from $20.7 to $20.1 billion from 2003 to 2004, some sectors, such as building sets and action figures, had experienced double-digit drops in sales in 2003. And while those traditional categories had firmed up somewhat in 2004, the main growth in the sector was coming from the nontraditional electronics side. In fact, the toy sector overall has been losing market share to video and computer games and consoles, products that are certainly about play, but not about toys in a traditional sense.

If struggling to maintain market share in a consumer niche with declining or flatlining sales hasn't been challenge enough for toymakers, they have also had to contend with upheavals in the manufacturing and retail sectors. The Far East, in particular China, has come to dominate toy manufacturing. Toys tend to be fussy and labour-intensive to assemble and decorate, and rock-bottom labour costs overseas have caused production to all but decamp from North America. By 2002, U.S. imports of toys made in China exceeded $12 billion, as companies either set up plants overseas or subcontracted the work to foreign factories. The manufacturing shift has been so dramatic that, in 2001, the U.S. trade association,

Toy Manufacturers of America, was compelled to rename itself the Toy Industry Association.

On the retailing side, the big-box discount operations, led by Wal-Mart and Target, have pushed down price points and profit margins for toymakers, while providing daunting competition for the established toy retailers with whom the makers had long-standing relationships. These were not only independents with shelves of hand-carved stacking blocks, but erstwhile category giants. FAO Schwarz, the venerated U.S. upscale toy retailer, failed after 141 years in business, filing for bankruptcy in early December 2003. Sears, in its effort to compete with the likes of Wal-Mart, created the KayBee Toys retail area within its mall stores, but the experiment failed. And no retail enterprise generated more negative headlines for the toy business than the flagship enterprise Toys R Us. Eclipsed by Wal-Mart as North America's number-one toy retailer, Toys R Us, a public company since 1978, found itself in aggressive retreat after a disappointing 2003 Christmas season. It closed down 182 Kids R Us and Imaginarium stores in early 2004. In August 2004, the company announced plans to separate its more profitable Babies R Us operation from the troubled Toys R Us chain. Finally, in March 2005, the entire Toys R Us company was purchased for $6.6 billion by an investment consortium.

That Toys R Us could find willing and eager investors is sign enough that the toy market is not a financial dead end. To be sure, nobody is predicting that children are going to stop wanting new playthings any time soon. And one of the consistent criticisms of the toy industry (and its massively consolidated retail sector) is that the products on offer lack diversity and imagination. Big-box retailing, so the knock goes, tends to exclude the small and quirky while emphasizing the entrenched brands—

products that best fit the price-point, inventory, and marketing-support demands of megavolume retailing. Any product sold in such a retailing environment is under intense pressure to meet revenue targets. There's little hope of building a following slowly. Shelf lives can be a matter of weeks if the retailer's projected sales figures aren't being met.

In toys, as in other product sectors, instant consumer recognition, which can avert many of the challenges of generating sales, is often achieved through branding strategies: New toys are introduced under the umbrella of an established product brand (such as Playskool or Hot Wheels), or are allied through licensing agreements with strong consumer brands—Disney's Winnie the Pooh, or the *Star Wars* film franchise, or the McDonald's restaurant chain, for example.

The industry overall can seem precariously driven by warhorses of the toy world. Many leading brands are several decades old; at Mattel alone, Barbie dates from 1959, GI Joe from 1963, and Hot Wheels from 1968. While these brands provide the desired consumer recognition, they must be constantly reinvented and updated to maintain market dominance. Mattel provided a glimpse of those challenges when it announced flat sales for the first quarter of 2005, its worldwide gross revenues hampered by a 15 percent decline in sales of the Barbie franchise and 2 percent in Hot Wheels.

The perpetuation, and revivals, of classics, which often counts on the retro aesthetic of parents who do the buying, testifies to the enduring power of the brand at an emotive level. But even perpetuating or reviving a particular brand, especially if it involves giving it a twist (as Ohio Arts did in 2005 by turning that low-tech laptop Etch A Sketch, into an entirely new version, Electronics ETO, which plugs into a television) meets the critical toy market test of novelty.

"Product life cycles are short, about six to eighteen months," Anton Rabie, Spin Master's co-CEO, explains. "Your competitive advantage comes from constantly introducing innovative products. Not always does a new product introduction need to be completely revolutionary. Sometimes it can be a twist of technology or a new feature to a proven play pattern." The kids market, he sums up, "is driven by what's new."

In the hall-of-mirrors of novelty, things can become so old that they become new again; products are dug out of trademark storage, dusted off, and taken for a fresh spin in the marketplace. It's happened with skateboards and yo-yos. Spin Master had one of its early successes in 2001 by updating Shrinky Dinks, a craft product from the early 1970s, and in 2005 it rode the wave of a revival of the Teenage Mutant Ninja Turtles franchise by introducing an action figures and accessories line as Fox Television brought back the cartoon.

Sheer novelty drives much consumer marketing. There would be no fashion industry without it. But the toy industry, and the greater kids market beyond traditional toys (which Spin Master increasingly has addressed in a quest to diversify so as not to rely on one product line for more than 20 percent of revenues) is like the rest of the consumer world on fast-forward. It is made even more hyper, more unpredictable, by fads, collectibles crazes, and the influence of product tie-ins through licensing agreements with pop-culture offerings of film, television, and music that are themselves prone to rapid changes in popularity. It's product development and marketing in the fast lane. And Spin Master has been able to deal with it through its commitment to alliances.

Spin Master embraces licensing: Its product line includes tie-ins with Disney, Nestlé, SpongeBob SquarePants, and Marvel

Enterprises, to name a few. (In 2005, Spin Master scored an Ultimate Toy Award in the activity category from the Toy Industry Association for its S'Mores Maker, a product concept brought to Spin Master by Funanuf with a brand tie-in with Hershey Foods.) And, to a far greater degree than the toy industry's giants, Spin Master also depends on third parties—inventors and brokers—to bring forward intriguing concepts that cut through the clutter of the marketplace. "We have such a large desire for growth," says Rabie, "we feel that if we can harness the world's ideas, we can grow faster than we would by growing on ideas developed internally."

"There's a core philosophy at Spin Master that's different," adds Ronnen Harary. "A lot of other companies don't like to share revenues or royalties. They'd rather carry the overhead, and generate the ideas internally, than pay 5 percent to outsiders. Our philosophy is: We don't mind paying for great ideas. We'll earn less margin in order to have great ideas in more categories."

It's that simple. But it's not that easy.

Measured by raw revenues, Spin Master is dwarfed by the big players in the toy industry. A privately held company, Spin Master's sales are eclipsed by the $3 billion of Hasbro and the $5 billion of Mattel (2004). But Spin Master has been able to turn size to its advantage. It is a lean operation, with all of its manufacturing outsourced. Even relying on outside inventors doesn't mean there's nothing creative going on. Spin Master has remained distinct in a business of multibillion-dollar corporations by having such hands-on executives who trust their instincts and are willing to move on opportunities with what is, for their industry, astonishing speed. Being able to capitalize quickly on concepts in a business so driven by novelty is a major competitive advantage.

Spin Master's alliance-oriented business model and entrepreneurial daring can move a new product to market with astonishing speed—and self-confidence. A prime example is Catch-a-Bubble, exemplifying Spin Master's knack for creating "category buster" products. These are innovative concepts that almost instantly become a segment leader, allowing Spin Master to take by storm a product niche in which it previously wasn't known at all. And once one successful product is out there, Spin Master's line often expands. In the case of Catch-a-Bubble, the company has gone from one breakthrough product to a total of five under the Professor Bubbles umbrella.

The Catch-a-Bubble success began with Peter Fish, an Australian toy maker and inventor. Fish recognized the potential of an invention by Jackie Lin of Taiwan. A polymer in a bubble solution caused rapid drying of blown bubbles, preventing them from breaking for at least several minutes, allowing them to be stacked and otherwise manipulated by a child's hands. It was an irresistible twist on a traditional child's toy. Fish secured world rights and introduced it successfully through his own company in Australia.

Fish then showed the product to Bryan Irwin of Canada's Irwin Marketing while both were in Hong Kong. He wanted Irwin's help in breaking into the North American market. "I convinced him he shouldn't do it on his own," says Irwin. "I gave him the names of three companies, but I said my personal preference was Spin Master." Irwin liked Spin Master's speed-to-market savvy, openness to new ideas from outsiders, and he knew the Spin Master principals well enough to arrange a showing quickly.

Irwin contacted Anton Rabie, who also happened to be in Hong Kong. A meeting was immediately arranged on January 10, 2002, which included Ronnen Harary and Jackie Lin, whose company made the bubble solution. "Because of our reputation for rewarding outside inventors and for powerhouse marketing," says Rabie, "Bryan convinced Jackie Lin and Peter Fish that we were the ones who could bring it to market faster than anyone." Two days later, a deal was struck.

The speed with which the product introduction unfolded was stunning. By mid-February, Spin Master had a full product presentation, complete with finished packaging, at the crucial New York Toy Show, at the same time that market testing was under way in Houston. Spin Master shot its own TV commercial and had it on the air by April.

"Our company likes to seize opportunities when they arise," says Harary. "That's the root of all things we do. We'll flex the organization to achieve those goals. You can't do it on every single product, but on key ones, we have. The infrastructure is there. People know that when the company gets behind certain items, they have to pick up the pace and get it done."

Orders were quickly, and massively, booked. Six months after the first meeting in Hong Kong, Spin Master had shipped seven million units and invoiced $15 million. The concept was so cool that *Wired* magazine wrote up the invention that June. *Time* magazine chose Catch-a-Bubble as one of its best inventions of 2002. One American retailer sold 100,000 units in a single week in December 2002.

A Christmas sensation most certainly is what toymakers are after: a product that breaks through the clutter of the toy aisles in the consumer's imagination and becomes a must-have item, sometimes even a cultural phenomenon. Before Furby in 1998, there was Tickle Me Elmo in 1996, and what remains the toy industry's sales supernova, Cabbage Patch Kids, in 1983.

Spin Master had its breakout experience in 1998 with Air Hogs, a product that brilliantly updated an old and unspectacular category—radio-controlled (RC) model aircraft—while moving it into the mass-market toy mainstream. RC aircraft, with their little gasoline engines, are a hobbyist specialty. They're definitely not a Wal-Mart product. Air Hogs made a wide sweep around the entire model-aircraft sector, forgoing the gasoline engine. The toy not only operated in the air, it *ran* on air. A clever motor was powered entirely by compressed air, and the compression was provided by a pump that a child could operate.

The concept had been brought to Spin Master in 1996 by two British inventors, who had already been turned down by fifteen companies. The Spin Master partners put in the many hours and prototype tests necessary to create a marketable product from a simple, alluring concept of an air-powered engine. The Air Hog was kid-friendly and cleverly designed from both an engineering and aesthetic perspective. It was cool enough to make adults sit up and take notice, garnering a high-five from *Popular Science* magazine. It unquestionably put Spin Master on the toy industry map, not only because of the end product but also because of the way the partners were able to work so effectively with independent inventors to produce an innovative product that fit the mass-market retail environment.

The trick with success in the toy business is to perform like an Air Hog, executing an impressive barrel roll with critics and consumers, and then, freshly recharged, doing it all over again. The alternative—to soar to spectacular heights, only to crash-land, or to prove otherwise to be a one-flight wonder—is a constant hazard in the industry. Witness the Cabbage Patch Kids phenomenon of 1983, which made Coleco an industry powerhouse. Five years later, Coleco was bankrupt, and the Cabbage Patch rights passed to

Hasbro and then to Mattel, the dolls a shadow of their former market presence.

Rapid-fire boom-bust happens to particular products in the toy business partly because popular culture works in such unexpected ways to anoint its latest sensations, and toys have peculiar cross-pollinations of success-fail factors. Sales are routinely buttressed by the cross-licensing of pop-culture trademarks, ranging from the real (professional sports) to the imaginary (characters from *Sesame Street, The Simpsons,* and various Hollywood films). The cross-licensing results can be literal—an action figure based on an athlete or film character—or incidental—an image of Winnie the Pooh printed on the back of a child's folding chair. The ability of these licensing deals to move product profitably depends on the added value the association brings to a particular product (beloved cartoon characters can help sell lunchboxes, but can they move more units of dental floss?), and to the strength of the licensed tie-in. Blockbuster films have become a key driver in toy sales, and 2005 was expected to be a particularly tie-in–dependent year, with the summer releases of installments in the *Star Wars* (credited with beginning the modern licensing era in 1977), *Batman,* and *Harry Potter* franchises. A toy brand already successful in its own right can find additional marketing heft through tie-ins, as Lego did with *Star Wars.* But such tie-ins are only as successful as the cultural brands to which a toy hitches its wagon. Where an association with *Jurassic Park* can prove to be brilliant, one with a big-budget bomb such as *Wild, Wild Wes*t can be anything but.

The context of purchase-making, which is dominated by the gift-giving of the Christmas season, means that what sells and what doesn't is affected not only by price point but by what a child desires ... and by what a gift buyer, most often an adult relative, wants that child to have. And because Christmas is an emotionally charged time for many, when a particular toy becomes hot, panic buying can set in as parents don't want their kids left out of a fad item. This panic can be further stoked by the collectibles craze, in which toys are purchased purely as a short-term (to meet retail shortages by offering items for sale on eBay at massive markup) or as a long-term investment.

Spin Master has found success producing toys (and more) by banking on familiar strategies that address the dynamics of this market: developing proprietary, expandable brand lines, offering collectibles products (as opposed to products that through unpredictable cultural hysteria become collectibles), and cross-licensing pop-culture brands. It has also managed to find success by working productively with the big-box retailers. And it has done it all in a way that has maximized its own flexibility.

The toy business is a perfect place to find the perfect example of a virtual company, because products, for the most part, are not created in corporate R&D centres. "For the entire toy industry," explains Harold Chizick, Spin Master's vice-president, promotional marketing, "the majority of inventions are from outside sources." Spin Master adheres to the outside-source strategy as much as, if not more than, any other company. These inventions are created by free-agent talents who earn their living this way, dreaming up new things to go under the Christmas tree, as well as by guys—and it is overwhelmingly a guy thing—who manage to hit on one clever, marketable concept while fiddling in their basement workshop.

Getting to these people, fostering relationships, making sure that they think of your company first when they hit on something novel and compelling, is the key to winding up with marketable product. It's not a model suitable for all industries that rely to a fundamental degree on invention—pharmaceutical companies cannot wait for somebody to call from Albuquerque, announcing he's just created a new anti-cholesterol drug therapy in his garage. And not all of Spin Master's idea development is so arm's-length—the acquisition in 2004 of Britain's Worlds Apart, responsible for the Marshmallow children's furniture line, gained it a staff of ten product designers. But for the toy business, Spin Master has shown that prioritizing freelance inventors works. The trick is to focus on the quality of the relationships with these creative allies, so that the inventions flow their way, and not to a competitor. Becoming a highly likely place for great new ideas to be submitted—ideas that cannot even be anticipated by Spin Master—has been a key part of the company's growth strategy.

Such relationship building includes another important source of concepts: brokers of existing products, like Funanuf. It's eminently possible for toys to make their successful debut in Japan and Europe and remain unknown in North America. Unlike innovations in electronics, children's products don't always easily cross cultural borders. But a surprising number of seemingly culture-specific phenomena make the leap—witness how the Yu-Gi-Oh! craze was so readily exported to North America from Japan. Spin Master does scouting of its own in overseas markets for products with potential. But it also relies on solid relations with brokers to bring to them products with breakout potential.

Becoming the highly likely place for new ideas to arrive involves far more than being able to boast of a demonstrable success. Air Hogs, for example, was—and continues to be—a showcase success, but it would be meaningless if inventors didn't feel they could be dealt with fairly. Independent creative talents, particularly those with one great idea per lifetime, can be leery of corporations, fearful of losing their invention outright to an unscrupulous operation, or of having the opportunity squandered by poor marketing. (That said, Spin Master doesn't as a rule deal with back-of-envelope concepts. Ideas that it seriously considers developing into a marketable product are usually fairly advanced as prototypes.)

"We've kept our integrity," says Chizick. "We deliver on promises. We support products through advertising. We say we'll do something, and we follow through. We take inventors on retreats, and make sure they see that we recognize their importance to our success. So much of the business depends on intangible relationship building."

The retail sector is an enormously important partner in Spin Master's business. Most of its sales are made not only *through* the big-box retailers but *to* those retailers. The business is not consignment-based, like the book trade, nor does it require the manufacturer to rent shelf space, like the grocery trade. The retailer purchases product from Spin Master and takes it into inventory.

Companies that don't sell product directly to the consumer but, instead, to dealers are sometimes in danger of forgetting who, ultimately, is the customer. The U.S. auto industry in the 1970s was criticized for becoming overly focused on producing models that the dealer network wanted, and not what the consumer was increasingly interested in buying; this short-sightedness began the shift toward the domination of Japanese imports. Fundamentally, dealers and vendors are supposed to know what customers want, but the nature of their retailing methods and price-point and inventory demands can mean that they favour a product that suits their business model, rather than product a consumer is actually interested in buying. Retailing can also be hobbled by a rearview-mirror mentality, making decisions on what will be stocked for the coming season based on what sold well in a previous season. It's a situation that cuts across the experiences of many creative enterprises. At worst, it stifles innovation and causes both the product's producer and the retailer to miss out on consumer trends. Capital and energy consumed by tired concepts could have been employed profitably (and with potentially no greater expense) in developing novelty.

How do producers and retailers alike avoid this trap? The best approach is highly calculated risk-taking. With a company such as Spin Master, much of the sense of a product's potential comes at that gut level: Like the record producer who once described his job as twiddling knobs in a studio until the noise coming through the headphones made his hair stand on end, toymakers know that great product has an undeniable, almost unquantifiable, *zing*. Retailers can appreciate that zing, but it is still very difficult to predict how well a particular product will do in a business that is so dominated by the fourth-quarter sales of the often fad- (and angst-) driven Christmas season. It's even more unpredictable in the area of collectibles, which Spin Master entered in 2003 with Mighty Beanz. "With the potential sales for a collectible," Chizick explains, "you don't know how high is high, and how low is low."

Spin Master learns everything it can about a product's potential before bringing it to retailers. If the product is brand new, it looks to other products (either its own or those of competitors) in the same category to gain insight into what its sales potential will be—

clues that have already been factored into the decision to bring its new product to market. If the product has already made its debut in another market, sales numbers there are a logical basis of planning. With Tengamo, for example, Spin Master could point to the sales of more than seven million units just in Denmark. Multiples can be worked up for new markets and provided to retailers as evidence of potential sales.

But there's no substitute for actually going out and testing the waters with a product, which is a challenge in a Christmas-driven retail sector. While toys do sell year-round, a general rule is that anything with a retail price of more than $20 is a Christmas item. The retailers do their ordering in May and June, and take product into inventory in August in preparation for the holiday season. To help retailers make decisions on how much of what to order, Spin Master employs what it calls an inventory management system (IMS), which is essentially pre-Christmas test marketing. A product is introduced in the spring to one or more city markets. Enough product is provided to satisfy the local retailers. Advertising and promotion is focused on the test market; it may involve television spots and promotion samples. It's a good dress rehearsal both for retailers and Spin Master. The company learns how enthusiastic a sample market is for a product, and also what works and doesn't work in the way of promotion. Based on unit sales in that test period, the retailer can place orders for the crucial Christmas season with far greater confidence.

"Where other toy companies simply supply stores," says Wong, "I think Spin Master can almost be seen as partner to them, advising them on what's going to be hot and why. And I think stores listen to Spin Master more because of that. Even if they don't buy the Spin Master product, time spent talking to Spin Master is time well spent for them. When you come out with successive hits the way they have, the stores start saying, 'Geeze, these guys really know something.'"

Working with retailers in test markets paid major dividends in 2003 with Mighty Beanz and in 2004 with Bella Dancerella. They are very different products. Mighty Beanz were Spin Master's foray into the volatile collectibles market, while Bella Dancerella, an instruction-activity product for young girls, was a departure in its own right.

Anton Rabie came across Mighty Beanz in a toymaker's showroom in 2002, and they gave him a dose of what he calls the "warm and fuzzies." They were relatively inexpensive novelty items, a plastic version of Mexican jumping beans decorated with collectible individual characters arranged in teams (a licensing tie-in with the NHL was inevitable). At the time, America's youth were laying down about $19 for a pack of Yu-Gi-Oh! cards. A pack of five Mighty Beanz would command $5.99. Spin Master signed a licensing deal for North America with the rights holder, Australia's Moose Enterprises, then test-marketed Mighty Beanz using the IMS strategy in Chicago and Los Angeles in July 2003, supporting their introduction with local advertising on specialty children's channels such as Nickelodeon. It took only a few days for local stores to sell out. Pretty soon, as the Mighty Beanz general release turned into a generator of about U.S.$60 million in Christmas sales in 2003, desperate collectors (and parents) were trying to buy must-have Beanz for over $100 on eBay.

Bella Dancerella was introduced in 2004 as a home ballet studio aimed at girls ages three to eight. It features a double-sided ballet mat with a barre and a thirty-minute instructional video. A tutu and slippers package is also offered. Given the target age range, the product's emphasis is on fun, with children engaged through the video in singing and playing while learning five basic ballet positions. It received the IMS treatment in Chicago that May, carried by Wal-Mart, Target, Kaybee Toys, and Toys R Us. "Even at a $30 price point, we're selling more than ten pieces per store per week. That's a monster result for that price point at that time of year," says Chizick. The IMS trial helped turn Bella Dancerella into a bestseller for Spin Master, not to mention for the retailers that committed to orders.

The success of Bella Dancerella underscores for Wong the importance of a gut-instinct enterprise such as Spin Master making its own calls on what will sell, rather than waiting for marketing studies to deliver feedback from consumers on what they're interested in buying. "You can't ask the customer to describe something like their ballet product, but once you see it, you say, 'My daughter would love that.' Air Hogs was similar. When you're playing the game of what's hot twelve months down the road, you need to be like the quintessential art connoisseurs. You don't know what's good, but you know what you like."

There's another "partnering" lesson to be learned from the success of such product market tests and launches: media buzz. Media reportage can't be purchased, and buzz can occur only if a buzz is generated in the first place, but admiring press coverage and earned media exposure (as opposed to exposure that's paid for through advertising) can have an enormous impact on a product launch. No one in the toy business has ever forgotten the lesson on the power of a charmed media to move product that was delivered by the Tickle Me Elmo craze of 1998. A plush battery-powered Elmo doll giggled when tickled: There wasn't much more to say. This toy spinoff from *Sesame Street* wasn't doing anything spectacular, sales-wise, until a sample was sent to Rosie O'Donnell, who had a one-year-old son and was at the height of her daytime TV talk show power, with an audience of stay-at-home moms with young kids. Once Rosie showed off the doll on camera and threw free ones into the audience on successive shows whenever a guest said the word "wall," the public went into an Elmo feeding frenzy.

Spin Master hasn't quite achieved that earned exposure nirvana, but it has done well not only through local media coverage of IMS tests but also through admiring recommendations by arm's-length media outlets. In the case of Bella Dancerella, the IMS in Chicago received a nice boost from an article in the Weekend Plus section of the *Chicago Tribune,* which also gave generous coverage to Spin Master's IMS trial of Stink Blasters, three-inch-tall dolls licensed from rights-holder MEG in California, which, well, emit an array of noxious odours when squeezed. You might say the coverage raised a bit of a stink.

Early in its history, Spin Master recognized the critical role of licensing agreements that secure tie-ins with sales-critical brand associations. Today, Spin Master's food products line features the award-winning S'Mores Maker, as well as *The Simpsons* Squishee Maker, and (with the McKids brand of McDonald's) the McFlurry Maker and Triple Thick Milkshake Maker. The Mighty Beanz collectibles line alone features license tie-ins with Marvel Comics, *The Simpsons,* and the National Hockey League.

"Our licensing department started up six years ago, with no experience, but with common sense," says Chizick. "We read up on the licensing industry, and built that part of the business through relationships and trust. It turned us into a world-class licensing department. Children's furniture is a licence-driven business. And licences are so competitive. It's what's caused the

Marshmallow brand to grow the way it has. Everything is about alliances, about allying yourself with the greatest partners in those areas."

Forging such brand licensing alliances is another area where intangibles are important. "I was working recently with Nestlé on a cereal promotion, for the global market outside North America," says Chizick. "I'd been to Lausanne, and now my counterpart was coming to Toronto. He'd never been to Canada. I said, 'Stay an extra day and I'll take you snowmobiling.' We try going the extra mile so that when we have a proposal on the table and everything is weighing out equally with a competitor, we're the first choice."

But Chizick knows that snowmobile rides in Muskoka alone aren't going to close the deal. "We want to be seen as that choice because we have a great batting average, and have integrity as a core value."

"I do find there's a tremendous amount of integrity and honour with them," says Fuhrer. The attrition rate in toy concepts, he notes, is extremely high. Many ideas that inventors and brokers such as Fuhrer come up with never get past the pitch to the company. And some of them die before they reach a store shelf. "I've presented something to Spin Master and they've made a decision that they'll proceed. Then they'll decide it doesn't fit what they're doing. But they make good on whatever they said they were going to do. They're very reliable. It's almost as if they sit down in a room and say, 'What is the right thing to do?'"

So far, the right thing to do has been what they've been doing all along. To Wong, Spin Master is an excellent example of an enterprise that keeps doing the right things because the principals keep having the conversations that people like him and Fuhrer can so easily imagine happening. And they do happen. "In all of these successful entrepreneurial companies," says Wong, "they have the good sense to stop every once in a while and ask, why is it working? Whether it was planned or not in the first place, they recognize that what they're doing is smart. They talk about what's working and what isn't. Even though they might have stumbled onto the magic ingredient, they're smart enough to recognize the font of their success."

The Deloitte perspective

Pursuing and managing alliances, acquisitions, and other strategic relationships

For partners Ronnen Harary, Anton Rabie, and Ben Varadi, strategic alliances were an imperative to growth in a market dominated by several behemoths. They were astute enough to recognize that their organization did not have all the new product ideas it needed, nor did it have the resources to produce them. But by leveraging the intellectual property—the ideas—available through the world's inventors and rights holders (i.e., the network of inventors) and developing alliances with key manufacturers in Asia, the company was able to:

- Produce innovative, demonstrably different products for its market.
- Execute a cost-effective growth strategy, based on access to resources on a pay-per-use basis.
- Exercise control over "creative development"—a core competency of Spin Master.

In a business where ideas are the lifeblood of an organization and copy-cats can get to market before the original, "speed to market" is a major strategic advantage enjoyed by Spin Master. The alliance model, combined with Spin Master's best practices for reducing the product development cycle, have allowed the company to capture the hearts and wallets of its customers with its powerful brand, before knock-offs can have a meaningful impact.

Key factors that Spin Master has proven to be exceptional at evaluating with regard to its alliances are:

- Compatible goals: Spin Master and its partners share a similar vision.
- Cooperative cultures: Building relationships and understanding your partner and culture.
- Complementary skills: Partners must contribute something that the other does not have and enjoy a benefit from the relationship.
- Commensurate risk: Both partners need to share the possible downside or risk from the alliance.

Most alliances/partnerships fail—it's a fact of business life. Companies can improve chances for success by executing some key steps:

- Develop a well-thought-out alliance strategy (Why are we doing this? What do we want to accomplish?).
- Identify and evaluate possible partners and alternative partnership arrangements.
- Perform extensive due diligence on partners' management team and business.
- Clearly outline role, responsibilities, and expectations up front with a partner.
- Implement organizational and technological infrastructure to support the alliance with specific financial and operational metrics.
- Build the relationship with the partner on trust and a common purpose.

3 Getting the ingredients right

Managing the risks associated with growth

Boston Pizza

Canada's 50 Best Managed Companies winner, 1994–2002
Named to Platinum Club 2003

It's the beginning of the lunch hour trade, and the customers are just starting to file into the restaurant. They have the choice of making a left-hand turn into the sports bar, or turning right, into the dining area. Our customer chooses the dining room, a combination of booths and tables. TSN is on the television monitor mounted high in the room's corner. The sound is off, and the dining area's stereo system is layering a profile of hockey legend Bobby Clarke with the dance groove of Gwen Stefani. The decor is bright and warm—perhaps "lively" is the word—and consistent with the restaurant's target markets: families and young adults. The stainless steel gleam of the open kitchen is visible, but separated from the dining area. Service is prompt, delivered by a confident, well-dressed fortysomething woman, not a kid working part-time.

She's pleasant and solicitous without being unctuously familiar, and the food—a Caesar salad and a new addition to the menu, a Thai noodle entrée—is well prepared, well priced, and not what you'd expect from a restaurant with "pizza" in its name. The customer is in a hurry and manages to order, eat, and settle the bill in thirty minutes, though he didn't feel rushed by the staff.

This is Boston Pizza in the spring of 2005. It sure isn't Boston, and you sure don't have to order pizza. The new franchise, on Highway 12 in Midland, Ontario, on southern Georgian Bay, shares a development pad with two consumer heavy-hitters: Tim Hortons and Wal-Mart. It's a detail that would not mean much to the average restaurant-goer, beyond the fact that there's lots of parking and the location is accessible. But the company the restaurant is keeping, in the form of the world's largest retailer and Canada's slam-dunk champion of the fast-java-fix, says much to any analyst of franchising. It shows that the restaurant concept has arrived—after one false start—in central Canada. It has managed to break through the "Boston what?" reaction of many property developers and reached the A-list of suburban locations.

It was much harder to do than most people would expect, even for a highly successful franchise chain founded in Alberta in 1964, and which had about 130 restaurants in western Canada when it decided to expand eastward. It took two tries, and it proved to be more difficult, even on the second, successful effort, in a way the company didn't expect at all.

The restaurant chain didn't start in Boston. Nor was it inspired by great pizza in Boston. And no, the name wasn't hit upon through extensive marketing analysis. The original restaurant in Edmonton was founded in 1964 by two Greek immigrants—Chris Petropavlis, who was already running a pizza-and-pasta restaurant in Calgary, and Gus Agioritis, who was making aluminum windows and doors in Edmonton and wanted to get into the same business as Petropavlis. They teamed up to open the Edmonton operation, which was basically a Greek restaurant that also served the relatively novel food format known as pizza.

Stories vary about how they ended up with "Boston" in the name. One version is that they had a few other ideas, but the names were already registered, and so they fell back on "Boston." Another version is that "Boston," to their minds, was the only choice there ever was. Either way, it was picked because it was the name of a big American city and sounded worldly, and had associations such as Boston cream pie, and, especially, the Boston Bruins of the National Hockey League.

Here is the odd and even capricious thing about the Boston Bruins inspiration: in addition to the Bruins being a struggling team at the time, perennial cellar-dwellers in league standings, Edmonton had long been the stomping grounds of the Detroit Red Wings, which sponsored the Edmonton Flyers of the Western Hockey League. But in the summer of 1963, the Red Wings summarily suspended their sponsorship of the minor-pro club, and the Flyers had to shut down. But for that decision, one has to conclude, there might be over two hundred restaurants today called Detroit Pizza.

So then, why Boston? A telling clue: back in 1957, the Red Wings had dealt away to Boston (for Terry Sawchuk) one of the great home-grown hockey talents of Edmonton, left-winger Johnny Bucyk (who in the late 1950s played on Boston's "Uke" line with Vic Stasiuk, who came out of Lethbridge). Two years before Bucyk was made the Bruins' captain, Petropavlis and Agioritis's Edmonton restaurant opened as Boston Pizza and Pasta. By 1970, when Bucyk led the Bruins to their first Stanley Cup, the restaurateurs had seventeen outlets in western Canada. The big, bad Bruins by then had Bobby Orr and Phil Esposito, and Boston Pizza was on a roll of its own.

Jim Treliving was a young RCMP officer in Edmonton when he started working part-time as a bouncer at a local Boston Pizza in 1966. He left the force in 1968 to open a franchise with a partner, Don Spence, in Penticton, British Columbia, then another, and another. Their accountant, George Melville, got in on the act by becoming a franchisee in his own right in 1973. Petropavlis and Agioritis sold the company to an Edmonton franchisee, Ron Coyle, in 1978, who changed the name of the business to Boston Pizza International Ltd. In 1983, Boston Pizza was acquired from Coyle by Treliving and Melville, who raised capital through silent partners who held half the equity, and head office was established in Richmond, British Columbia.

Securing a restaurant concession at Expo '86 in Vancouver ahead of Pizza Hut was a major boost to the chain's profile, and it soon acted to lever the exposure into international expansion, entering the Asian market in 1988 and moving into southern Ontario in 1989. Nine outlets were opened in Taiwan, Japan, China, and Hong Kong, three in southern Ontario. They were all closed by 1992.

The reasons for this reversal of fortune varied. The company blames the propensity of property owners in the Asia market to demand unrealistic increases when the short-term leases of restaurants came up for renewal. Ontario was beset by a number of problems, including consistency in food quality and collateral damage when the recession in the early 1990s hit the property developer with which the company had paired. But a significant reason was the lack of a corporate presence in the Ontario market to oversee the expansion. Boston Pizza would try again in 1997, and this time, would get it right.

In coming to Ontario, Boston Pizza was attempting to crack a consumer market that was not only numerically larger than the West but also much more crowded with competition. There had already been one failed attempt, but the company found itself at a crossroads that forced it to take another look. "We had to decide if we were going to be a western chain forever, or if we were going to go east and then south, into the United States," recalls Mike Cordoba, who had joined the company in 1993 and was promoted to CEO in 2004.

More than a few people in the restaurant business in central Canada felt that Boston Pizza had been taught an unforgettable lesson in its first attempt to expand into Ontario. The basic message supposedly was that Ontario was the big leagues, that Boston Pizza had been in over its head in a crowded, fiercely competitive market, and that it should just go home, lick its wounds, toss some pizza in the oven and some pasta in the pot, and accept its role as a regional restaurant phenomenon. The company felt otherwise, and it recognized from that first attempt an entirely different set of lessons than the ones Ontario restaurant pros thought they should have learned.

Ontario—and then Quebec, Atlantic Canada, and the United States—were felt to be more than doable as expansion territories for the company. A much different approach would be required from the first try at central and southern Ontario, but the restaurant chain itself had been evolving since that first attempt. And Boston Pizza had a strong grasp of the portability of its concept and where its market niche lay. As crowded and as competitive as the eastern markets were, they didn't have anything like Boston Pizza. The company understood the core strength of its product. It knew that some aspects of it would have to be adjusted for the new markets, but that the basic package would work. As it turned out, it has worked even better in the new markets than it did in the old.

Even though Boston Pizza had been around for almost twenty years when Treliving and Melville acquired it in 1983, their purchase was, in a large sense, the start-up point for the chain today. They had both been around the brand for some time, but as owners they made a critical decision at this stage. They owned sixteen restaurants themselves, which they decided to sell to franchisees. One restaurant was retained as a corporate outlet and used for training, but otherwise, Treliving and Melville committed themselves to running the parent company, and not confusing the situation by trying to be a major franchisee at the same time.

It was the beginning of a commitment to leave restaurants in the hands of franchisees and not have corporate outlets, beyond a handful used in regional training. There was a downside to the strategy. Treliving and Melville themselves note that a corporate restaurant can be run at a higher individual profit margin than one operated by a franchisee, which pays Boston Pizza a royalty of 7 percent on gross sales—so much so that one corporate outlet could realize as much profit for the parent company as the royalties from three franchise outlets. And some of Boston Pizza's most significant competitors operate at least partly on a corporate ownership basis.

Tony Dimnik, an accounting professor at Queen's School of Business, has known Boston Pizza since he visited one on his first date with his wife in 1969. "It really has evolved from a pizza place to a wide variety of food offerings, some of them very cosmopolitan. We were delighted when the Kingston location opened, and we go there on a regular basis." And so, while Dimnik's casual dining has benefited from Boston Pizza's eastward expansion, he has also come to consider its place in the classic tensions in corporate and franchise ownership models.

"You have to be able to balance the franchisee's efforts and initiatives with a franchise-wide standard," Dimnik says. "How do you ensure that the restaurant experience is the same everywhere for the customer? Unless you have enough control, you end up with a chain of independent stores, without the core characteristics of the brand."

Successful growth, Dimnik advises, requires a precise balance between three factors: the growth itself, control, and cash flow. Think of it as a three-legged table. Saw off one leg, and the whole thing topples. "If you have growth and cash flow, but no control, you lose the concept you had in the first place," he notes. "But control is no use if it chokes off growth or cash flow—perhaps because the necessary franchisees aren't attracted by the policies of head office, or because the company decides to retain ownership of all stores, but can't fund or manage the expansion properly.

"As long as business is growing, the tensions among the three factors can be managed. But if there's a bump along the way, franchisees start looking out for themselves, and that can be a concern." He gives the example of several chains where, "when things started to go bad, it was hard to make franchisees follow corporate policies. Everyone was looking out for their own interests."

From an expansion perspective, Boston Pizza saw a significant advantage to the franchise route: franchisees put up the investment capital and assume the risk of the new locations. Owners invariably have a more vested interest in the success or failure of an individual restaurant than does a corporate manager. And as an enterprise expands geographically, it is an asset to have owners on the ground in new locations who know the local terrain. For Boston Pizza, then, managing the risks associated with growth, especially when it accelerated with the expansion into central Canada and the United States, was anchored substantially in the franchising concept. This allowed the parent company, the franchisor, to concentrate on marshalling the myriad details of expansion.

The casual-dining segment of the restaurant industry has offered plenty of competition, some of it from Boston Pizza's own backyard. One of the largest is The Keg, a steakhouse chain created by Vancouver's George Tidball in 1971. It was purchased by Britain's Whitbread PLC in 1987, then, in 1997, acquired by Vancouver businessman David Aisenstat, who had been a Keg investor and director before the Whitbread purchase. More than eighty restaurants were in The Keg Royalties Income Fund as of the third-quarter 2004. (Like many of its chain competitors, Boston Pizza is also organized within an income trust.)

In 1990, the first Jack Astor's Bar and Grill opened in St. Catharines, Ontario. It is the largest in a stable of concept restaurants owned by SIR Corp., accounting for twenty-nine of about forty restaurants (which include Alice Fazooli's! Italian Crabshack and Armadillo Texas Grill, in Toronto's entertainment district).

Prime Restaurants has served up more competition, mainly through its flagship East Side Mario's, of which there were 106 by 2004. With most of its restaurants located in Ontario, and a similar target market of "families with kids and adults wanting to enjoy good food in an exuberant atmosphere," East Side Mario's was an entrenched competitor for Boston Pizza as it looked to expand into eastern Ontario, as well as a fresh competitive threat in its own backyard as East Side Mario's focused on western Canada in its growth plans. (Sixteen had opened in the West by 2004.) Prime also owned Canada's "original roadhouse," Casey's Bar & Grill, founded in 1970, which had about three dozen outlets by 2004.

Then there is Cara Operations Ltd., of Toronto, with a formidable portfolio of restaurant brands, including two casual-dining competitors of Boston Pizza it wholly owns: Kelsey's Neighbourhood Bar & Grill, with 111 restaurants in Canada and New York State; and Montana's Cookhouse, whose 53 outlets are aimed at young families. As a franchisee, Cara also operates sixteen Outback Steakhouse restaurants, and owns 74 percent of Milestone's Grill & Bar, which has 22 restaurants offering upscale casual dining. Also in the competitive mix, albeit leaning toward the fast-food segment, are the venerable Pizza Hut, Cara's wholly owned Swiss Chalet, and, out of Quebec, the St-Hubert rotisserie chicken chain.

In short, the market was crowded when Boston Pizza decided to have another try at central Canada, and was certainly more crowded than when it had launched the previous attempt. Competition was tough, and experienced operations such as Cara could approach the restaurant pie one slice at a time, with fine-tuned concepts for different market segments and dining experiences, a strategy also being pursued by SIR Corp. with its concept restaurants. (The industry was also headed for a triple whammy of negatives: 9/11, which affected travel overall and impacted on restaurants that relied on tourism; the SARS scare, which hit hard Toronto-area restaurants, again because of the tourism decline; and finally, the mad cow outbreak in Alberta, which did no favours for restaurants dependent on steak sales.)

But for all the heavy traffic of established and emerging competitors, Boston Pizza was confident it had a unique concept.

"Bar and grill" occurs over and over in the names of these casual-dining themes, but Boston Pizza had created a restaurant layout with two distinct areas, closed off from one another: the dining room and the sports bar. "Our competitive advantage is in the physical structure of the building," affirms Cordoba.

It's not unusual to find a bar in a casual-dining restaurant, but that bar is usually open to the dining area and often serves as a pre-meal staging zone, where customers wait for their table to become available. Boston Pizza, on the other hand, had created two distinct profit centres under one roof, each serving specific clientele and diversifying the revenue opportunities. They also produced four "day parts," according to Cordoba, as opposed to the traditional two of lunch and dinner.

"Our competitors do about 70 percent of their revenues at lunch and dinner," says Cordoba of the traditional sit-down restaurant revenue model. "We do 55 to 60 percent in those times, but we also do a great business in the sports bar," which he says generates 25 percent of a typical restaurant's business, particularly in the 8 P.M. to 3 A.M. period. The company's strategy for building business in the sports bar is to aggressively court local amateur sports groups. Boston Pizza outlets offer to come out to a game, tape it, and play it back on the big-screen television. "We go after recreational sports teams," says Cordoba. "We'll sponsor the whole league."

Another 15 percent comes from takeout, but Boston Pizza does not consider itself to be competing with traditional takeout and delivery operations such as Pizza Pizza, nor has it been moving toward more of a takeout–drive through–curbside pickup model being embraced by the likes of Swiss Chalet and Pizza Hut. "We don't offer discounts," notes Cordoba. "We do high-end packaging for takeout. The idea is to give you the experience of the food that is in the restaurants."

The Boston Pizza menu is what Cordoba calls "intensified" pizza and pasta. And the food is good. But it was the multi-dimensional restaurant experience (rounded out by summer patios) and the target marketing to sports groups that gave the company a competitive edge. Like Boston Pizza, both East Side Mario's and Casey's sponsor local sports organizations to help generate table traffic, but according to Cordoba, "We didn't see anybody in Ontario doing it consistently, going after nontraditional business. But we had to educate the consumer that we're not just lunch and dinner."

Even before making its second run at central Canada, the company decided it needed to more aggressively communicate the Boston Pizza experience. In 1993, it launched its first major television marketing campaign, and it did so by allying with one of the most recognized faces on prime time television.

The idea was proposed by Mike Cyr, then director of sales and marketing. Cyr suggested they hire as a spokesperson actor John Ratzenberger, who had played one of the most beloved characters in sitcom history: Cliff Clavin, the mama's boy postman with a head full of useless information, in the long-running hit *Cheers*. The show, which first aired in 1982, had made its final telecast on May 20, 1993. *Cheers*, of course, was set in a Boston bar.

"The first campaign traded a little on the Cliff Clavin persona," says Stephen Plunkett, vice-president, marketing, who joined Boston Pizza in 1997. "It was difficult, because John didn't own that character and it couldn't go that far." But he had the Beantown accent and the face recognition.

In the first television commercials, Ratzenberger appeared inside a Boston Pizza, reading letters to the company and providing know-it-all, Clavin-like responses. In one, he answered a letter from his mother, which was as close as he could come to playing his *Cheers* character. In 1996 and then again in 1998, Ratzenberger played a detective—Ratzenberger P.I., the "P.I." standing for "pizza investigator"—who investigates Boston Pizza and learns that there's more to the restaurant than just pizza.

Indirectly allying the chain with *Cheers* was risky, as the sitcom bar was a cellar-dwelling watering hole filled with oddballs drinking away their sorrows, not a family restaurant—although the sports bar connection was there to be made in the back of the audience's mind, through the bar's owner, the Boston Red Sox reliever Sam Malone. Another risk was that by 1998, the beefy, silvery-haired Ratzenberger was fifty-one years old, on the outside edge of the desired customer demographic. But the spots worked. They won several advertising awards, and the $100,000 fee per campaign that Ratzenberger commanded was considered money well spent. Plunkett has called the Ratzenberger initiative "a turning point for selling the brand. It moved us into a totally different place."

The brand, in fact, was becoming so well established that the company had to aggressively defend it.

As the Boston Pizza chain expanded and strove to build brand recognition, the company could not afford to have that recognition diluted or confused by rival restaurants. The "Boston" name was sacrosanct, and the company made aggressive efforts to protect its hold on the trademark.

It was not going to be easy, as the "Boston" label had been used widely by restaurateurs—just the way Chris Petropavlis and Gus Agioritis had in Edmonton back in 1964. But Boston Pizza had built up a considerable market presence since then, and it needed to ensure that no one else entered the Canadian market with a rival "Boston" concept. Defending the trademark would earn the franchisor a place in case law, and a court confrontation with an arm of one of the largest restaurant companies in the world: McDonald's.

Back in 1988, Boston Pizza International had been successful in denying trademark protection to Boston Seafood House Ltd. But its big legal struggle began in 1995, when it took on Boston Chicken Inc., which had registered its trademark in Canada in 1992. Boston Chicken was the U.S. restaurant franchising sensation of the 1990s. It had started in Boston in 1985, and a partnership that acquired it in 1992 set out to conquer the American appetite through rotisserie chicken from an intital base of 34 stores. After an IPO in late 1993, Boston Chicken became an investor and business-press darling, and expanded rapidly. By the end of 1994, it had not yet reached Canada, but had opened 530 outlets in the United States. At that point, Boston Pizza had 93 restaurants in five provinces. With industry observers crediting Boston Chicken with being smarter at the franchise restaurant game than McDonald's—company officials proclaimed that its chicken was the new pizza, and senior executives were drawn from Blockbuster Video, Pizza Hut, KFC, and PepsiCo Restaurants International—Boston Chicken was giving Boston Pizza more than a little cause for concern. On April 3, 1995, Boston Pizza applied to the Federal Court of Canada to expunge the trademarks Boston Chicken had registered in Canada.

Boston Chicken proved to be a moving target. As the chain rapidly expanded, so did the menu, to the point that chicken was being perceived as a brand problem. And so, beginning in February 1996, Boston Chicken restaurants began morphing into Boston Market, and the number of stores surpassed 1000 that year, with a total of 3600 by 2003 being predicted. But by 1997, dissenting voices began to be heard about its accounting methods as serious profitability problems with franchises were revealed. From there, the Boston Chicken–Boston Market boom quickly went bust. Crushed by debt and overexpansion, Boston Chicken Inc. filed for bankruptcy protection in October 1998. In December 1999, McDonald's announced its plan to purchase the assets of Boston Chicken, which included the relevant trademarks for Canada, which were assigned to McDonald's' subsidiary, Global Restaurant Operations of Ireland Ltd. As a result, Boston Pizza found itself tilting with McDonald's over trademark protection in Canada.

On the surface, the legal battle might not have seemed to represent particularly high stakes. It was widely noted that McDonald's had bought what remained of Boston Chicken not for the troubled restaurant concept but for the prime U.S. real estate the outlets occupied, and McDonald's was closing Boston Markets, not opening more of them. But the case was an important one for trademark law in general, and for Boston Pizza's ability to fend off market incursions by other "Boston" restaurant concepts. And McDonald's had entered the picture as a legal adversary just as Boston Pizza was beginning its fresh effort to expand into central Canada.

You only had to do the math to realize that taking the brand east was the future of the restaurant chain. By the time the trademark action was taken against Boston Chicken in 1995, Boston Pizza had ninety restaurants in western Canada, and three in northwest Ontario, in Kenora and Thunder Bay. With a combined population of just under 9 million, the western provinces were supporting one Boston Pizza for about every 100,000 people. Ontario alone was home to 11.4 million people. While there were more restaurant competitors in Ontario than in the West, it still was reasonable to extrapolate from the western growth experience a potential to add another hundred restaurants in Ontario. Quebec, with a population of 7.2 million, could follow, and Atlantic Canada and the United States also beckoned.

Things were going to be done a little differently for the second expansion effort into central Canada. There had been some key staff hirings at head office, including Mike Cordoba and Stephen Plunkett. In preparation for the thrust east, the company also brought onboard Mark Pacinda, a Connecticut native with an MBA from the University of New York, who had been president of the international division of Arby's in Toronto. He had turned down a move to Florida with Arby's and was about to accept a job with Citibank in Chicago when he was recruited in 1997 by Boston Pizza to oversee the eastern expansion.

The single most important decision Boston Pizza made in the renewed expansion was to have a strong corporate presence in the Ontario market. Trying to run the expansion from Richmond, British Columbia, the first time around hadn't worked. "We decided to set up an infrastructure," says Cordoba. "We hired people and established an office in Mississauga." In addition to having Pacinda in place, both as a senior company executive and someone experienced in restaurant franchising in central Canada, Jim Treliving personally signalled how committed Boston Pizza was to the expansion by relocating to Oakville and taking it upon himself to travel Ontario and really get to know it. "I had spent some time in Ottawa with the RCMP thirty years before," Treliving notes in *Partners in Success,* the company's corporate history. "But I had been in the west for thirty years. I didn't know what was going on in Ontario. It's just a three-hour time difference, but it's like a world away."

There was a significant cost associated with establishing the corporate presence in Mississauga, on the order of $1 million per year. But the expense was outweighed by the many advantages, and the built-in risk reduction. The company had to be on the ground, demonstrating its commitment to the expansion, which meant commitment to franchisees that their $500,000 initial investment was not being sunk into here-today, gone-tomorrow test marketing. Having a corporate presence, says Cordoba, "gave us the ability to use buying power nationally, but also to act locally. We had some leverage. But we had no brand awareness.

"We found that in Ontario, there's a lot more stiff competition, but there's also a larger population. A lot of concepts have survived and done well, because there's just more people. In Ontario, the key to success is getting mass quickly. And people didn't know who we were."

Boston Pizza meant nothing to most consumers, to the potential franchisee, and to developers on whom the company was relying for prime locations. If anything, a negative association from the earlier expansion effort lingered. Hadn't this restaurant concept already been tried here once, and failed?

With a corporate presence established, the main task, says Cordoba, "was to build up restaurants as quickly as we could, to get brand awareness and some reaction in the market."

Establishing the brand was not something that could be solved simply by wall-to-wall advertising: without restaurants in place, there was nothing to advertise. "You have to get people to come into the restaurant," Plunkett advises, "because that's where it all happens. Until people make the choice to come in and have the dining experience, it's all just talk. The challenge in southern and central Ontario was that there was some awareness of brand name, from westerners who had moved east, but nobody had seen a Boston Pizza restaurant in a long time.

"We had to establish our brand story: Who are we? What do we do that we think is particularly good? Pizza is a big differentiator. For a very low cost per diner, someone can experience the dining environment. They can then come back and try something else on the menu."

A corporate outlet was built in a prime location, at Winston Churchill Boulevard and the QEW in Oakville. Commuters in this heavy-traffic corridor in the Greater Toronto Area could not help but at least see the restaurant. But to create quickly an entire chain of restaurants in Ontario, Boston Pizza had two choices: continue in the Oakville mode and build corporate outlets, or work to attract local franchisees, the way the West had been won.

With many of its competitors in Ontario using the corporate ownership model, it would have been easy for Boston Pizza to adopt the same strategy, particularly since the chain faced an uphill battle in convincing potential franchisees in central Canada to invest in a concept they didn't know, when franchises in established brands were available. But Boston Pizza had been successful by sticking to what it knew, and it knew franchising, and it was committed to not confusing the roles of franchisor and franchisee. Expanding aggressively into a new market was challenge enough. It didn't need to complicate matters by also adopting a completely new business model.

Fortunately, Boston Pizza was able to establish the Ontario beachhead by turning to some of its existing franchisees in the West, who believed in the portability of the restaurant concept and were reassured by the franchisor's commitment to the new market. Three western franchise groups were instrumental in getting the brand established in Ontario. At the same time, Boston Pizza employed a new franchising strategy, one that had been used by Boston Chicken in its rapid buildup. Rather than depend on individual franchisees, this model assigns area development rights to franchise investors, with territories in Boston Pizza's case that can support between two and five stores. The idea is to build brand mass, and by 2004, Boston Pizza had assigned all fifteen development areas in Ontario, and was focusing from that point on single-restaurant franchises in the smaller markets between them.

Building brand mass also means building restaurants, and not just anywhere. Boston Pizza knew, going into the second assault on Ontario, that winning over developers was crucial. "Some developers knew us from the West," says Cordoba. "We needed to build up trust with developers. We did a lot of wining and dining to secure deals."

"Did we have to adapt the concept immensely?" Cordoba poses. "No. We had to localize to some extent in central Canada. Meatball subs, for example, are big in Ontario, but not in the West." The company did recognize that a new advertising campaign, with a new spokesperson, was in order. The Ratzenberger campaigns had been measurably successful in improving brand awareness, but by the turn of the millennium, Ratzenberger wasn't getting any younger, and while his voice continues to be well known from his work in animated blockbusters such as *Toy Story* and *Finding Nemo,* his main claim to fame, of postman Cliff on *Cheers,* was attached to a sitcom that had been known only through reruns for the better part of a decade. And so, in 2002, Boston Pizza turned to Toronto-born comic and actor Howie Mandel.

It is probably lost on most consumers who see Mandel in Boston Pizza commercials that he was a mainstay performer on the medical drama *St. Elsewhere,* playing Dr. Wayne Fiscus for the show's entire run, from 1982 to 1988, and moreover, that the drama was set in the fictional down-on-its-heels St. Eligius Hospital in, of all places, Boston. (A serendipitous moment of Boston Pizza promotion: Ratzenberger made a crossover appearance as Cliff Clavin on *St. Elsewhere* in 1985.) The *St. Elsewhere* connection to Boston was a fluke. "It definitely wasn't deliberate," says Plunkett. "For a lot of people, *St. Elsewhere* is a big reference for Mandel and his career; for others, it's the animated kid's show *Bobby's World*. And then for others, it's his club act that's best known."

It was far more important that Mandel suited the message Boston Pizza was trying to convey than that some connection to Boston could be winnowed from his resumé. "Like any other personality, you have to make sure that it isn't a forced fit," says Plunkett.

Mandel's appeal as a spokesperson is his non-threatening goofiness, his ability to come across as someone you'd actually encounter at Boston Pizza, kibitzing with friends and family. Mandel also has a good connection with kids for the young families demographic, being a parent himself and having worked in children's entertainment (indeed, Mandel was the creator of *Bobby's World*, which ran on Fox from 1990 to 1998). His persona has been a good match for the chain's demographics. According to Boston Pizza's February 2005 market monitor, the customer mix consists of families with children under age ten (30 percent), families with children over age ten (24 percent), adults ages nineteen to thirty-four (27 percent), and adults thirty-five and older (19 percent).

"The feedback I've gotten from people is, 'I think he's somebody I would bump into at the restaurant,'" says Plunkett. "And we do have a strong kids' program. A large proportion of guests is families with children. We do a lot to promote that within the restaurant environment. We hear that we do that well."

Mandel also conveys the madcap fun of late-night business. "When most restaurants are shuttered at midnight," says Plunkett, "we have a customer group, mostly young adults who are interested in being in a restaurant, or in a sports bar. It's a well-established part of our business in Alberta, and a growing part in our new areas. Ontario has a well-established set of competitors. But East Side Mario's and Kelsey's have also pushed west. The main difference for us, in moving into Ontario, is we have to establish ourselves as a sports bar environment."

For Plunkett, success is driven by making the best first impression possible. "The first visit is critical, if you're going to get them to come back. You create guest loyalty at the tabletop." And when Boston Pizza came east, finding people to prepare the food and bring it to the table was surprisingly difficult.

Boston Pizza fully expected to have its work cut out for it wooing developers and franchisees in the eastern expansion. And it also knew that it would have to learn the consumer quirks of markets beyond the Manitoba-Ontario border. But what caught the company completely off guard was the challenge in finding employees.

A typical Boston Pizza requires a staff of sixty to seventy. The company was accustomed to a new franchisee placing an advertisement in the newspaper and receiving one to two hundred job applications. But some of the new outlets in eastern Ontario weren't getting any applications. This problem was a direct consequence of a lack of brand awareness in the new market: People didn't know Boston Pizza the way they knew East Side Mario's or Kelsey's. And because Boston Pizza was looking for adults they could train to a high level of professionalism, and not kids looking to flip burgers part-time at any old place for minimum wage, it found itself having to convince prospective employees that Boston Pizza was an appealing career opportunity.

The company continues to work overtime to attract talent. Among the many strategies it has employed are attending university job fairs, employing recruiters, and paying its staff bonuses for bringing in new hires.

If there was a setback in the eastern expansion, it was the loss of the federal court case against the Boston Chicken trademark. On September 17, 2001, Judge Marc Nadon ruled that at the time the Boston Chicken trademark and logo were registered in Canada in 1992, "there was no likelihood of confusion between the applicant's trade-mark BOSTON PIZZA and the respondent's marks," and that Boston Pizza "has failed to meet its burden of demonstrating the likelihood of confusion." As Boston Chicken no longer existed as a restaurant concept, the ruling might not have seemed significant. In fact, it was critical to the interpretation in case law of how far trademark protection could extend in Canada, and would have consequences for Boston Pizza's ability to defend its "Boston" franchise brand going forward.

Boston Pizza appealed the outcome, securing a favourable ruling on March 7, 2003. The appeal court decision hinged on the issue of distinctiveness, and whether the Boston Chicken trademark could claim this distinctiveness before it was introduced to the Canadian market. The appeal court decided that the Boston Chicken trademark could not secure the necessary distinction without having been used in Canada. It was an important ruling, not only for Boston Pizza but for the franchising industry as a whole. American franchising concepts with names (and products) sounding similar to established Canadian ones would have difficulty coming into Canada with their trademarks unchallenged, even if those trademarks had established a strong brand presence in the United States, and there had even been some awareness instilled in Canadian consumers through the cross-border spillover effect of media advertising.

The court success became far less academic for Boston Pizza when McDonald's began reviving the Boston Market concept, the successor brand to Boston Chicken. Even before the appeal ruling was received, a significant threat had arisen on the Boston Market front. McDonald's had continued to operate Boston Market outlets in the United States, and in October 2001, plans were announced for the opening of three in Ontario in association with McDonald's Restaurants of Canada. In August 2002—with the first two Boston Markets opening in Ontario in September and December—Boston Pizza sought an injunction to prevent the restaurants from using the "Boston" name. The Boston Market side launched its own attempt to have trademarks stripped from Boston Pizza.

Boston Pizza held on to its trademarks but was unsuccessful in its request for an injunction. A principal reason the court turned down Boston Pizza's request for an expungement of the Boston Market trademark was that the judge was satisfied the restaurant concepts were sufficiently dissimilar: Boston Pizza was in the business of casual dining (and in fact had the dominant market share in Canada), while Boston Market, lacking full table service, was in the takeout (or what the industry calls the home meal replacement) trade.

As it happened, the Boston Market experiment in Ontario was short-lived, as McDonald's closed the three restaurants soon after. And on January 7, 2005, Boston Pizza was successful in having Canada's Trade-marks Opposition Board deny McDonald's Global Restaurant Operations of Ireland Ltd. a trademark for "Boston

Market," accepting Boston Pizza's argument that the name would be confused with its own.

Boston Pizza had twenty-one outlets in Ontario when it moved against Boston Market in 2001. By early 2005, Boston Pizza had opened a total of forty-five, and was moving into Quebec, Atlantic Canada, and the United States.

If any new market requires abundant risk management measures for a western Canadian restaurant company, it is Quebec. It must come to terms with a different language, different cultural conventions in dining—a business environment far more different from the rest of North America than Ontario is from Alberta. Boston Pizza planned methodically for the move into Quebec, and did not rush the process.

"We spent a year and a half doing market research," says Cordoba, "and we've had to make a lot of adjustments." The table turnover rate is lower, as patrons linger over their meals, even at lunch. The wine list requires more variety, and salads and entrées need to be served separately, rather than on a single plate. But even at that, Plunkett points out that the restaurant design is exactly the same in Quebec as elsewhere. "It's fair to say that the business model and strategy behind how we market the brand is fully portable. There are only three new menu items in Quebec and an expanded wine list."

As with Ontario, Boston Pizza took care to establish a separate business management unit, in Laval in 2004, and hired bilingual staff. It also chose to build a corporate restaurant in Laval, as it had in Oakville, to serve as a training centre and to raise brand presence in greater Montreal. A start-up specialist, Wayne Shanahan, a bilingual native of Quebec City, was hired to run the business unit, and he in turn brought in Mike Kaburis, who had been in charge of restaurant operations for St-Hubert, to do the same job for Boston Pizza.

And while all this was going on, Boston Pizza was moving into the U.S. market. With the Ontario expansion unfolding properly, Jim Treliving left Oakville, relocating to Dallas in 2000. By then there were already six U.S. outlets, which for trademark reasons were operating as Boston's the Gourmet Pizza. Expansion in the United States has been greatly assisted on the developer front by working closely in new developments with AMC Theatres, a major U.S.–based megaplex theatre company. The Atlantic Canada market was also breached in 2002, with the first outlet opening in Halifax.

Success in expansion, says Cordoba, "is about doing your homework the best you can, and not taking a closed-minded approach. You have to expect the unexpected, and be prepared to modify your strategy, but without throwing it out."

While Boston Pizza does secure some consultation from outside the company, its strategic planning is essentially internally driven. It has a solid grasp of its own strengths, and of the core characteristics that make the product competitive, and it assesses the position and strength of competitors in new markets. "We have a lot of internal systems," says Cordoba, "and with them, did a lot of work to assess growth, and what the challenges would be. It turns out that in central Canada, our unit economics are better than in western Canada. We're getting better real estate deals now."

"It's going well now," says Cordoba, "but it's been a hell of a challenge."

The Deloitte perspective

Managing the risks associated with growth

Boston Pizza's steady and well-managed growth strategy has resulted in it becoming one of North America's top franchises. This successful strategy is evident by the annual growth in restaurants and plans for continued expansion. Boston Pizza's management team is extremely qualified and has a proven track record in growing the number of outlets and providing franchisees with the necessary support to operate a successful restaurant. Dining experiences at Boston Pizza locations, whether they are in Vancouver, Toronto, Yellowknife, or Montreal, are consistent in food quality and service, which is an indication that the company's expansion plans have been properly implemented.

Significant growth initiatives such as Boston Pizza's inevitably raise a few questions for owners and managers:

- Is our risk assessment process robust enough to address key business decisions?
- Do we have the processes and metrics to monitor and evaluate the impact of risks taken?
- Do we have the strategy to maximize the gains from the risks we take?

Along the way, particularly after the initial, unsuccessful attempt to establish the chain in Ontario in the late 1980s, Jim Treliving and George Melville learned that perhaps the answers to some of these questions were not yes. The good news is that, like all good owners, they and their management team learned from their experiences and made their processes addressing expansion and risk more robust and effective.

Other enterprises that are confronting the risks and complexities of expansion and growth are well advised to follow these guidelines:

Conduct a risk assessment to identify, evaluate, and address the risks of a new initiative:

- Define the rationale for the new initiative.
- Identify the company's strengths and weaknesses.
- Perform a risk analysis to determine whether the initiative is aligned with the company's risk parameters.

Develop a detailed business plan:

- Develop the company's business plan with measures to manage risks.
- Agree with all the stakeholders on the strategy developed to address the risk.
- Set milestones to reassess the risks and adapt the plan over time.

Execute the plan and adapt:

- Appoint an implementation team and identify appropriate responsibility.
- Create the processes of monitoring, reporting, and controlling the risk.
- Refine the plan periodically based on the primary results.

As with Boston Pizza, those who undertake the planning, research, and risk analysis, and produce an in-depth business and implementation plan, will avoid costly mistakes and enjoy financial stability and a proper alignment of the company's risk to the organization's strategy.

Capability

4 Beyond bricks and mortar

Capitalizing on technology solutions

EllisDon

Canada's 50 Best Managed Companies winner, 2002–2004

Geoff Smith has a way of saying things that raises eyebrows, and sometimes hackles, in his industry. "I am of the view that the construction industry is behind the times," he offers. "It's not servicing clients. It's confrontational with them. As an industry, we were not changing. You're starting to see it play out. Companies that do adapt will survive and grab market share. Those that don't will be out of business. If you don't grab the opportunity, you're gone."

Smith can say this with a large dollop of *mea culpa* on behalf of EllisDon, the company of which he is president and CEO. The Mississauga, Ontario–based general contractor has undergone a significant shakeup in its outlook and corporate culture in recent years.

The company was founded in 1951 in London, Ontario, by two brothers, Donald J. and David Ellis Smith (hence EllisDon). They had four employees, and their first job was a house addition, which the company likes to note came in on time and on budget. Just five years later, EllisDon was the first Canadian construction company to purchase and operate its own tower crane. In 1986, the company secured a landmark contract, the design-build for Toronto's SkyDome (now the Rogers Centre); two years later, it completed the $500 million CAMI (General Motors/Suzuki joint venture) automotive plant in Ingersoll, Ontario, the largest such plant in North America to have been created under a design-build contract with a guaranteed price.

Other showcase projects include the National Gallery of Canada in Ottawa and London's Canary Wharf, and more recently, EllisDon was selected as the preconstruction manager for the redevelopment (to a Frank Gehry design) of the Art Gallery of Ontario, slated for completion in 2008. It has also built up a large portfolio of health care projects—probably the largest in Canada—and has worked on airports and educational institutions. It has built in thirteen countries. It established an office in Saudi Arabia in 1974; in 1993, it was the first Canadian construction company to work in Latvia and Lithuania, after the fall of the Iron Curtain; and it secured its first project in Malaysia in 1997. It developed a taste for the Olympics when it built the athlete's village for the 1996 Atlanta Games, and is proud of the fact that for the problem-plagued 2004 Athens Games, it contributed the athletes' medical clinic and the basketball and fencing facilities without drama.

Amid all that construction, EllisDon underwent a major renovation of its own. It began with a succession in the late 1990s, with the retirement of founder Donald J. Smith. The family's second generation bought the company, with Geoff Smith, a lawyer who practised outside EllisDon for two years before joining the company in 1982, holding the largest single block, 25 percent. (The company is 95 percent employee owned.)

"There was both a perception and a reality that EllisDon had become too traditional, too stuck in old ways, a perception of it being an old-fashioned, confrontational general contractor," says Geoff Smith. "Competitors were perceived to have moved ahead. We had a 'reputational' and maybe even a cultural problem inside."

One response was to assemble a new management team, with an independent board overseeing it. At the same time, a group inside EllisDon was given the task of assessing the challenges at hand. "The group thought hard about it, and felt the industry had its own issues around client service," says Smith. "We began looking for new ways to break out of it, and also to improve the industry's performance."

One way to break out was to institute a new, customer-focused policy, which EllisDon branded as Client First. It was designed to serve as the foundation of the renovated company's corporate culture. The policy includes a Client Charter of Rights, attached to every contract, as well as a Code of Conduct for EllisDon employees to follow.

It was also clear that a significant component of the breakout lay in technology. And not in traditional construction technology, such as earth movers and cement mixers. It was in internet-enabled software, a realm in which construction companies weren't as a rule particularly savvy. That EllisDon found such a solution is noteworthy in its own right. What is astonishing is that after doing such a terrific job of creating its own software solution, called EdgeBuilder, the company decided to create a whole new standalone business in order to place this competitive edge in the hands of its own competitors.

Like other general contractors, EllisDon had been rattled by the recession of the early 1990s, which slashed the number of construction start-ups. The contraction in the industry at the time had significant downstream consequences. As builders such as EllisDon reined in operations, young talents either moved on to other fields, or didn't enter their particular field to begin with.

And when construction recovered, EllisDon and many competitors were confronting a profound disconnect from one of the most transformative technologies of any century: the rise of the internet. Communications were being radically rewired (and unwired), and the impact went far beyond chat rooms and blogging. Internet protocol programs and devices were changing the way communications networks were structured, within companies and between them and their client bases. Databases were being interconnected, accessed, and interpreted in entirely new ways, with profound gains in operating efficiencies.

"I can't overplay the importance of the internet," says Bruce Fleming, EllisDon's vice-president and CIO. "We have to share a lot of information with a lot of people, inside and outside the company. It provides a cheap way to communicate with job sites. Three thousand contractors interact with us on a weekly basis, on projects involving fifty to sixty clients and several hundred consultants. But an internet-based solution wasn't available to us until the late 1990s."

General contractors weren't known for embracing the leading edges of technologies that didn't involve digging holes or assembling I-bar. EllisDon could lay claim to certain technology milestones in its industry. It says it was the first general contractor in Canada to fully computerize its accounting and cost control systems, in 1968, and in 1990 it established the industry's first free-standing R&D department, to stay on top of construction technology. But the building business generally was not keeping pace with the technology revolution in communications. In the 1990s, Fleming suggests, "The progressive ones had fax machines."

The disconnect from the internet within much of the construction trade coincided with the return to employment ranks of young white-collar workers as business rebounded. They had come of age in the new communications environment, and they expected that they would find it alive and well in the corporate world of a company as large as EllisDon. But they didn't. "Young people were coming in and saying, 'Where are these tools?'" says Fleming.

Coupled with the internal pressure of new, young staffers were the increasing expectations of customers. "Clients were wanting more transparency, better, more detailed reporting, and a much closer relationship," says Smith. "We were being asked about our systems by clients. We had good cost control systems, but not strong, transparent reporting systems."

"We were stretching to say that we had the systems in place," says Fleming.

At that point, Smith made a fateful decision about how to respond to these intertwined pressures. He needed to come to terms with what new tools EllisDon could employ in the area of project management and reportage systems. The usual corporate response would have been to turn to the company's own IT people. Instead, in 1999, Smith brought in one of EllisDon's top engineers.

"I sat down with Bruce, an engineer, *not* with the IT guys, on this issue," says Smith. "We pulled Bruce out of what he was doing, a very important role in critical engineering duties on major projects. I asked him to go and find out what was available in the marketplace, to buy it, and get it going. That was the original plan."

"Among the things EllisDon did well was to pick someone from the business side to drive the project, not a technology person," says

Elspeth Murray, associate professor of strategy and new ventures at Queen's School of Business. "That was critical."

Fleming was an interesting combination of traits: a structural engineer who also had an MBA, and a firm believer in what computers could do for his company. "I was pretty enthusiastic, maybe naively so," says Fleming. "I thought there must be some project management tools available."

"Bruce came back after four or five months," says Smith. "He had analyzed all the systems, and said there wasn't one out there."

"We just didn't see anything that met the mark," Fleming adds.

That result was fairly surprising, not to mention disconcerting. An industry involved in billions upon billions of dollars in construction in North America alone, each project generating mountains of documents—forms, correspondence, quotes, contracts, schedules, purchase orders, architectural drawings, drawing revisions, photographs, meeting minutes, payroll time sheets, permits, safety inspection reports, and anything else one could think of with respect to building structures in a way that involved clients, consultants, and innumerable subtrades—*this* industry did not have any kind of off-the-shelf software platform available to it, and nothing that Fleming concluded was particularly adaptable to its needs. "And even if there was one," Smith notes, "we wouldn't control it. If its developer didn't continue to innovate, we'd be stuck. So I presented a budget to begin EdgeBuilder."

"Building it internally, you rarely see that these days. The project was hugely risky for the company," says Murray.

A construction company was suddenly in the web-enabled software business. It had volunteered to dig what could have been a bottomless pit of corporate resources.

"One of the things we looked at way back in the project was getting a consistent approach to the work we're doing," says Bruce Fleming. "A typical $100 million job produces in a month ten thousand pages of outgoing documents, and about five thousand pages of incoming material. We've been able to handle that in a more effective, more consistent way." Fleming has noted that "our business is not data. It is documents and reports." In the process of creating EdgeBuilder, he found that on one job, only forty thousand of a hundred thousand documents generated were not a duplicate, and those non-duplicates included documents documenting the movement of documents. In addition to getting a handle on the paper storm, "We can now set metrics against how our people and subcontractors are performing, how they're handling questions, and addressing deficiencies," says Fleming. "Improving our performance would have been almost impossible before this system came along. From day one, that's what we thought we could do."

The review of EllisDon's needs had begun in midsummer 1999. By December, with the realization that there was nothing on the market that would do the job the way that EllisDon wanted it done, the development of EdgeBuilder began. "It was a pretty exciting time," Fleming recalls.

"Too many projects like this are led by a company's technology group," Fleming observes. "But you can't teach technology people the business. You have to act as a translator for them. A lot of systems we looked at were accounting systems. They didn't have business people in charge. You have to start out with where you make your money, and you work your way back from there."

"Before Bruce started developing EdgeBuilder," says Smith, "he did a lot of detailed consulting inside EllisDon. He and I also picked six clients, and six or seven designers and other consultants, and found out what they needed. We had terrific input. Bruce took all that information, put together a team, and hired programmers on contract."

"We started with two software developers," says Fleming. "When you don't know the direction in which you're heading, you need to keep the team small and figure it out first." By June 2000, Fleming "had a rough and ready prototype. It was an evolutionary process, putting things out early before it was ready for commercial use. We got some colourful feedback."

"We couldn't afford to do a full mock-up test," Smith elaborates. "We used our own people on job sites to test it. We kept *thanking* them for cooperating. We'd have management meetings, explaining to them where we were going, what the future looked like, so they could see the sky's-the-limit opportunity."

Notes Murray: "One of the great things about what EllisDon accomplished is that, in one of the most backward industries from an IT perspective, it was able to create a state-of-the-art system in the face of a long list of reasons it wouldn't be able to: no experience of its own, an industry that generally didn't use that kind of technology, and a culture that says, 'Give me a new excavator over information technology, any day.'"

It became more than a software project. "EdgeBuilder is the process by which project managers and superintendents manage all the documentation and communication on a project," Smith sums up. "It changes completely the way you work." EdgeBuilder naturally became a catalyst for change in the corporate culture of EllisDon, and in the practices of associated enterprises in the general contracting industry. It ramped up the introduction of computers, wireless personal digital assistants (PDAs), and the internet to the working lives and business processes of many people and organizations which were otherwise unaware of—or sometimes even hostile to—the new information age.

"One of the nice things about the general contracting business is that it is built on individual projects," says Fleming. "Processes as a result don't have to change midstream. We could introduce EdgeBuilder one project at a time. We started to roll it out on all new jobs on January 2001. The whole company was using it by 2003."

EllisDon had also been prescient enough to launch the EdgeBuilder project on the eve of a serious challenge for its industry in the area of performance bonds. "Every construction company needs to put up a performance bond from a large insurance company to guarantee the price on a project," Smith explains. "Especially since 9/11, there has been a terrific crunch. A lot of insurers and reinsurers got out of the market. It caused a major problem for construction companies and clients." The problem was exacerbated by Enron's reliance on performance bonds to guarantee future delivery on power contracts. When Enron went down, the fallout in the surety business was calamitous. Many reinsurers exited the business altogether, while others greatly reduced their number of clients.

EllisDon itself was hard-pressed in the area of performance bonds because of a long-standing problem with a luxury hotel–timeshare resort it had developed in St. Lucia—its decisive handling of which during the coincidental development of EdgeBuilder helped earn it a repeat appearance in the 50 Best Managed Companies list in 2003. Launched in 1989, Windjammer Landing had accumulated ponderous debts for EllisDon and kept losing money through the 1990s. The resort was an unattractive asset for surety bonding companies, and when the travel business was sideswiped by 9/11, things began to look dicey for the construction side of EllisDon, so much so that it was in danger of losing its ability to acquire bonding.

EllisDon management rapidly turned around Windjammer Landing, rebuilding its timeshare business, paying down the resort's debt (and refinancing it without any need for a guarantee from the parent company), and turning the resort from a money-loser into an operation with profits in 2004 in the millions. Even so, EllisDon still sought an advantage in the strained bonding market. "We saw that we had to demonstrate an edge to bonding companies on cost and project management," says Smith. EdgeBuilder had arrived not a moment too soon.

"As a company, we had little technology when we introduced the system," says Fleming. "There was only one mail server. Now we have a whole platform handling a hundred projects at any one time. Payroll time sheets are now electronic."

"It was like building a railway," says Smith. "We created a network that tied in a lot of other things, including web cameras, fax servers, messaging, and handhelds and remote devices. Geoff now has all the senior managers using BlackBerries. Five years ago, people couldn't even use computers. It's incredible, the changes that have happened.

"It was part of a huge cultural change we were putting the company through with respect to the way we deal with contractors, subcontractors, and clients," emphasizes Smith. "We were changing EllisDon from viewing itself as a construction company to being a service company. People got into the business because they like to build. But we're not builders. We're in a service industry that builds. We don't actually build a lot ourselves—the subcontractors do."

"EdgeBuilder has been really important for EllisDon," Smith adds. "Part of our success with it was because we gave it a brand name. It was important to market it, and have people rally around it. It has branded us as an innovative, forward-thinking company, and as far as a construction company can go, as a 'cool' company. It's been very helpful in attracting new talent, the young people coming out of school. It's made us look like a company on the move."

EdgeBuilder is now part of course curriculum in the construction program at Georgian College in Barrie, Ontario. And its use in EllisDon has given the company the confidence to extend greater responsibilities to young employees that they may not have been given otherwise. It is far easier to decide to give someone authority for a project more complex than one they've ever handled when you have EdgeBuilder providing management with a transparent overview of how a job is coming along.

EdgeBuilder was designed to organize and make accessible all materials related to a particular project. It became far more than text files and drawings, incorporating time-lapse webcam images and video-conferencing files. Using the internet, authorized participants can log in from anywhere in the world and examine materials on a particular project, and create new files within it. EdgeBuilder also automatically tracks workflow. "It has an online and offline functionality, which is one of the features we liked that we couldn't find elsewhere," says Fleming. "It couldn't be unusable half the time. External users interact through a browser, but our folks can go into a meeting with all the project files."

Surprisingly, EdgeBuilder was not universally welcomed by clients, who were supposed to have the most to gain from an efficient, transparent project management system. "It was very interesting to see which clients embraced it and which ones resisted it," says Smith. "Once you use a transparent system like this, it's wide open. If you don't know where it's taking you, you fear it and resist it. Some would embrace it enthusiastically, while others would resist it. It was the same way with design and contracting firms. Some grabbed it as a way to make themselves more efficient, while others saw it as a threat."

Yet, EdgeBuilder was so impressive that it earned the Diamond "best in show" prize at the Canadian Information Productivity Awards in 2003, with Fleming himself earning the CIO Canada Award. As Paul Nelson, CIO of Vision Mobile, who chaired the awards jury, told *CIO Canada* magazine, EllisDon's project "jumped out from a lot of the other entries because of its productivity gains. It helped EllisDon change their business substantially. The company grew more than 50 percent and they didn't have to increase their staff, and costs went down a bit. That's pretty substantial."

"The kind of technology investment that EllisDon made can give you a significant competitive edge, which might be temporary, but can still make it very hard for others to catch up," observes Murray. Fleming has had no difficulty measuring the impact of EdgeBuilder on EllisDon's performance. "Our revenues have grown predictably, from $600 million at the start of the project to just under $1.1 billion in the current year [2005], to what we expect to be $1.2 billion for 2006. Profit has grown at a better rate. Head office overheads have not gone up at all. There's been no additional staff. People are working incredibly hard, and the systems are working. Our legal costs are down 16 percent, and they've declined in a period of growth in the business. We have fewer clients, but we have retained them. Sixty-six percent of our current base is repeat clients. Our field staff has grown 66 percent, and they have to be immersed in and understand how we operate." EdgeBuilder has played a major role in ensuring that's happened.

EllisDon created EdgeBuilder fundamentally to give it a competitive edge in a highly competitive industry. Which is what makes, at first glance, its decision to make EdgeBuilder available to competitors such a head-scratching surprise. If Honda invented a zero-emissions engine that ran on water for ten cents a day, would it start selling those engines to General Motors? Why did EllisDon not grasp EdgeBuilder as tightly as possible, and lever its uniqueness as a demonstrable competitive edge?

Certainly the possibility of EdgeBuilder's use migrating outside EllisDon began to emerge early in the development process. "When we started to show prototypes, internally and externally, we found that everyone was having the same challenge," says Fleming. "I spoke at eight industry forums, and people said to me: 'Is it available for sale?' More overtures started coming from our own competitors."

Part of the drive to turn EdgeBuilder into a stand-alone enterprise with a product available to the entire industry came from the nature of the construction industry. Every project involves a network of independent trades and professional enterprises—a fact that made EdgeBuilder so necessary. These independent entities go on to tackle other jobs, many of them at the same time as a job with EllisDon. Once they became accustomed to working within EdgeBuilder, and realizing its advantages, they naturally wanted to be able to benefit from it when working with other general contractors.

And while it was true that EdgeBuilder could give EllisDon a performance advantage over other general contractors, the company couldn't possibly bid on every construction project in every community in North America and beyond. The competitive edge, in other words, had a finite edge, beyond which there was no advantage to EllisDon retaining exclusive use of EdgeBuilder. There was a world of general contracting beyond EllisDon's operating sphere that could benefit greatly from EdgeBuilder, and which increasingly appeared to be willing to pay for it.

"We had a terrific debate around here, which has pretty much subsided," says Smith. "It was: Is EdgeBuilder something you use internally to differentiate yourself from competitors? Or does it allow you to broaden yourself as an enterprise?" What had started out as an internal technology solution project had turned out to be a new product.

"We decided to offer it more broadly to the industry," says Smith. "The real reasons for me were twofold. First, there was potentially a lot of money to be made. Second, if we didn't do it, we'd be into a situation like Beta versus VHS."

Demand for a product such as EdgeBuilder was such that somebody inevitably was going to create a marketable rival. If EllisDon didn't act quickly and decisively to make the product available, an upstart could take the market away from it and even make EdgeBuilder obsolete, because clients would be accustomed to using the rival version. EllisDon would have devoted all that time, energy, and dollars to creating EdgeBuilder, only to be forced to adopt a product created in response to it. "We wanted to be the standard," says Smith.

But selling EdgeBuilder wouldn't simply be a matter of letting the construction industry know that the product was available. As Fleming bluntly puts it, "It's a fiercely competitive business, and people don't always like each other." EllisDon's general-contracting rivals—and there can be mutual dislikes in the business that verge on venal—weren't necessarily eager to become a customer of a company against which it regularly bid for work: A company as a rule does not turn to a rival for help in improving its competitiveness. EdgeBuilder would have to be spun off into its own business so that potential customers could be comfortable they were dealing with an organization held at arm's-length from EllisDon. And so a separate company was incorporated in the United States. "It has its own profit and loss responsibilities, its own president and management team, and operates in a separate location," says Fleming.

Initially launched in association with telecommunications giant BCE, all EdgeBuilder data now are hosted at IBM Global Services. The product supports more than a hundred clients, who use it on an application service provider (ASP) model. It's a clever approach, leasing usage rather than selling the software as a product, and one that Murray applauds. She also gives EllisDon top marks for having the sense to spin EdgeBuilder off into its own stand-alone enterprise. "What's remarkable about EllisDon in this case is the way it moved outside its core business to set up EdgeBuilder. A lot of companies wouldn't even recognize the value of the technology to its own business, let alone the opportunity to build a new business around it."

Even with EdgeBuilder's arm's-length structure, EllisDon recognizes that there is hesitancy among its general-contracting competitors to turn to it for a technology solution. "A couple months ago," says Smith, "we signed up on a trial basis a company we'd been competing against for forty years. They were as hesitant to buy it from us as we were to sell it to them. So we just said, 'You'd better be the best EdgeBuilder out there.'" Just because this company adopted EdgeBuilder didn't mean it and EllisDon couldn't continue to be fierce competitors.

Now that EdgeBuilder is up and running, the inevitable question it raises is, what's next?

EllisDon has moved to redefine itself within its industry as a service provider, not an old-style builder. EdgeBuilder has shown how far beyond the traditional parameters of backhoes and concrete this company is willing to go. Can cutting-edge information technology continue to be a part of the EllisDon brand?

Murray hopes so. "Now that it has this knowledge and expertise in IT," she proposes, "how are they going to leverage that in the future? Will it be in RFID [radio frequency identification] or some other technology? Is EdgeBuilder just one unique moment in time, and then boom, it's back to business as usual?" For a company nervy enough to create a transformative IT tool in an industry that wasn't even sure it wanted computers on desks, somehow EdgeBuilder doesn't feel like the edge of EllisDon's willingness to push boundaries.

The Deloitte perspective

Capitalizing on technology solutions

Most organizations—but particularly service companies—have long struggled in their quest to 'crack the code' on a technology solution that can deliver differentiated value to its clients. While EdgeBuilder may not yet be the industry's Holy Grail of project management, it has certainly differentiated the company in the minds of its clients. But perhaps as impressive as the development of the product itself is the thoughtful, professional process that management employed, particularly as software development was not then a recognized core competency.

Developing a significant software tool such as EdgeBuilder, and making it part of your corporate culture, requires excellent planning and execution. Keys to success for EllisDon, and for any company wishing to take a similar path, can be summarized as follows:

> **Business driven, technology supported:** EllisDon defined the business problem to be resolved in its industry, then confirmed that definition and the associated requirements with internal and external clients to ensure there was a clear understanding of the business objectives and drivers. Although technology was a major component of the overall solution, IT did not drive the project but instead supported the enabling of the business solution. By dedicating the resources from both fields, the greatest assurance is generated that the project stays on track to meet the business drivers.

Leading and managing the change initiative: The change in business process and level of technology utilized by EllisDon and its associates was enormous. Through its early prototyping, incorporating feedback from actual job site users generated not only the required input to ensure the product would be effective but also produced the enthusiasm and buy-in for the product. EllisDon achieved the required cultural change while also rallying support to the point of driving the attraction of new talent to, and interest in, the brand.

Continuous improvement: EdgeBuilder has initiated improvement and change far beyond its initial objective of addressing specific business issues and operating efficiencies. EllisDon has leaped forward in its integration of technology and communication with outside contractors and consultants. It captured the "sky's-the-limit" ideas and continued to incorporate and roll out these capabilities. Too often, clients succeed in the implementation of technology but then fail to continue through to improvement activities. EllisDon continued to such a degree that it actually reinvented EdgeBuilder, transforming it from an internal competitive differentiator to a stand-alone enterprise with a product that the company feels could become an industry standard. EllisDon achieved that goal by rolling the solution out in stages: an early rollout of the prototype to the end-users, followed by the rollout of the finished product, one project at a time, with continuous improvement at each stage.

5 Service, tailormade

Building and sustaining a customer-focused approach to sales and marketing

Harry Rosen

Canada's 50 Best Managed Companies winner, 1998–2000

So often, the key to successful retailing is seen from the perspective of location: Real estate is central to success or failure. Is the store on the right street? In the right neighbourhood? In the right mall? On the right floor of that mall? There's an underlying premise that the consumer world is flowing past like a river, and that the proprietor need only divert the stream through a well-positioned door to reap the greatest possible sales.

Location is indeed critical to most retail enterprises. But as customers flow in through a well-positioned door, so they must flow out. They come in, they browse; at a high-end menswear retailer, they might buy anything from a gift necktie to a $4000 made-to-measure suit. And then they leave. The sales staff of such an operation might well wonder if they'll ever see these same shoppers again. The owner might not be concerned, so long as a steady stream of new faces glides through the doors every day. But an experienced and successful retailer like Harry Rosen Inc., which understands location, can testify to the critical importance of knowing those faces—not every one of them, to be sure, but a significant number.

"My father built the business one customer at a time," says company CEO Larry Rosen. He's striving to continue doing the same thing, except that his customers add up to many, many more than the satisfied ones who patronized Harry Rosen's five-hundred-square-foot tailor's shop that opened on Parliament Street in Toronto's Cabbagetown district in 1954. Harry—who is still with the company he founded—could keep track of his clients in a notebook. Larry has about four hundred thousand customer names on a contact list, gleaned from sales at sixteen stores (fifteen retail, one outlet) in seven Canadian markets, and of them, a hundred thousand especially matter. They're the sweet spot of men's retailing: By the Rosen chain's definition, professionals with household incomes of at least $100,000 per year, spending $5000 or more on their clothes over a three-year period, who have been active as customers for the last two. These are the "clients," the cream of the "customers."

Larry emphasizes: "We're not an elitist organization. It doesn't matter what you look like, you're going to get the same level of service. A great salesperson doesn't prejudge." That's become especially important as the chain has moved into the twentysomething market. You can see the sales associates giving browsing time and room to young men who look like they just wandered in from a hip-hop concert.

Even so, while the Rosen chain aims to please everyone who walks through the store's door, whatever their needs, the company understands that a minority of the foot traffic in any store on any given day is at the heart of the enterprise. They must be catered to with special care, and their numbers must be replenished. Focusing on their needs has allowed the chain, by its estimate, to capture 35 to 40 percent of the market for "better quality menswear" among Canadian households with $150,000 or more in income.

Many people in retailing—in most avenues of business, in fact—understand the principle that not all customers are created equal. All other distinguishing quirks aside, a few very often outspend the many. But it can require a leap in strategic planning to orient an enterprise to that principle. Not simply to recognize it, but to cement it into the foundation of a business plan. However successful the Rosen chain had been, however solid the customer-service philosophy its founder gave it, the company still had to figure out how to turn an essential lesson—all customers are important, but not every customer is a client—into an approach to retailing that is quantifiable, actionable, and profitable.

The general retailing world has become driven not by one-on-one relationships with customers but by price points and volume turnover. The resulting churn can set in on all sides of an operation. Product is moving off the shelves at speeds that satisfy revenue-per-square-inch-per-day objectives. Inventory management systems are replenishing the shelves with just-in-time precision. But something disconcertingly similar can occur on the human side of the enterprise. Staff turnover can be high: They may be low paid, not well trained, not particularly motivated, and implicitly not particularly valued. And the customers are understood collectively, according to the flood of spending they generate, not as individual consumers. They're chasing bargains, or spending only when they're otherwise motivated to do so. They may have their main allegiance to brands, for which they can hardly be blamed, because that's what the retailer pushes as its price-point bargains, but these brands can be found at any number of rival enterprises.

Sales help can be hard to find, and even where there is help, the turnover means they're here today, gone tomorrow. The front-line staff aren't generating their own clients, a knowledge base that can encourage repeat business through customer satisfaction. And sometimes staff are so undertrained that the customer gets the feeling that earning a commission today, not meeting the customer's needs both now and over the long term, is the whole point of the attention they're receiving. Where the volume turnover of staff is a concern, shoppers can be made loyal through consistent savings, but they can also be lost when rival operations find a way to offer the same or comparable goods at yet lower prices.

Retailers can know a tremendous amount about the goods they sell, and they're learning more all the time, by employing technology such as radio frequency identification (RFID), which uses electronic tags to track items or shipments through the supply chain. Far more difficult to know much about is the individual customer. Privacy issues place limits on what, and how, data can be gathered and employed. But it's difficult for a business to know its customers if the customers don't have a particular relationship with the business—if the business hasn't been defined for them by more than weekly specials on brand items.

The hoary business adage of "knowing the customer" has not died along with hands-on mom-and-pop retailing, nor is it limited to boutique operations with a discrete clientele. The idea of defining and prioritizing service to a core customer base cuts across a variety of enterprises and business sectors. Retailers identify important customers and cater to them with special events and discounts tied to volume spending. The hospitality trade has recognized that certain travellers generate a disproportionate number of accommodation nights, or have specialized patterns, and target them with tailor-made promotions. Business travellers are especially lucrative because their trips are not discretionary; unlike vacationers, they have no choice but to be in certain places at certain times as part of their work, and a hotel chain can secure the lion's share of their accommodation spending if their needs are properly assessed and their dollars persuasively stretched for them.

Almost without exception in business, it is far less expensive—and ultimately more profitable—to retain a customer than to replace one. The quest to achieve high customer satisfaction so that those customers are retained pays dividends throughout an enterprise. It's what ultimately drives excellence at all levels, and the expense of achieving that excellence is more than compensated not only by revenues but by averting operating costs associated with customer turnover. The savings are realized in advertising, in product promotion, in loss leaders, in refunds, "make-goods," and warranties, in sales calls and business travel. If the cause of customer turnover is dissatisfaction with the product or service, the expense of remedying those problems is compounded by the promotion costs necessary to counter a poor marketplace image and rebuild sales as well as the customer base.

Companies of all kinds that rely on repeat business have been learning to make the most of what they can glean about their customer base, and to change business practices so that such knowledge is used effectively in increasing customer satisfaction, along with profitability. In the case of Harry Rosen, some old-fashioned values in customer service were dressed up in the shiny new clothing of electronic databases. The cut may have changed, but the fabrics were the same.

The original Harry Rosen outlet on Parliament Street defied the principle of the importance of location in successful retailing. It was a little out of the way. Most customers had to make a point of paying a visit. But this was not a business being built on walk-in trade. Nor was it selling butter and flour. Harry was selling quality menswear. The customer didn't need to be able to pop in once a week. Harry just had to make it worth their while to visit, and then expand his customer base through referrals. He did so through the classic combination of quality and service, and a large dollop of salesmanship.

In 1968, the Harry Rosen business—which by then consisted of a single store on Toronto's Richmond Street West—was acquired by the clothing retail giant Dylex, and, before long, Harry was running a mid-market menswear chain for Dylex, Tip Top Tailors. "With very little organizational experience, I was appointed the general manager of the Tip Top operation inside of a couple of months," he told *Canadian Business* magazine in 2004. "Tip Top was founded on such integrity and quality. And the product was still good. But it had no sense of quality about it, it had no sense of real style about it. Inside of a few months, I gave that business a direction." Made-to-measure menswear was so different from "bespoke," or tailored, menswear, and then again, not. "It's still a question of the quality of product you have, how you communicate it, who's your customer, and how do you plan to sell to that customer."

After running Tip Top for seven years, Harry returned to his namesake operation, acquiring 49 percent of it back from Dylex in 1975. Under the Dylex umbrella, the Harry Rosen chain expanded across Canada. Meanwhile, son Larry was earning an LL.B. and an

MBA from the University of Western Ontario. After practising law for a spell, he joined his father in the business in 1984, working his way up from buyer to regional director to vice-president to general merchandise manager, then to president, and finally to CEO, in 2000, after the death of Bob Humphrey, chairman and CEO of the venture since 1997.

"The business was very seat-of-the-pants entrepreneurial for many years," says Larry. "It expanded rapidly in the 1980s. It wasn't planned. We had the Midas touch. Everything went well. Being associated with Dylex helped in negotiating leases, in transportation, and in other ways. Then, in the early 1990s, the recession hit. We were in a few unwise locations, with five or six bad stores. Dylex was going through problems."

In January 1995, Dylex secured court protection from its creditors as it restructured. In 1996, the Rosen family teamed up with Bob Humphrey to acquire the 51 percent of the chain still owned by Dylex. Today, Harry Rosen Inc. is privately owned by the Rosens.

Larry had joined the senior management of Harry Rosen in 1990, and as the chain struggled to emerge from the crush of the recession and the overexpansion of the 1980s, it became clear that something new to the organization was in order. It was called strategic planning.

"We discovered the tools that allow executives to plan," Larry explains. "We started looking at where we wanted to be in two to five years. We looked at the skill sets of our associates. We set goals and measured progress. My father and Bob Humphrey had the vision that allowed us to adopt strategic planning. We've now pushed that planning down to an eleven-member management committee. We ask, What are our goals? Where do we want to go? We hire an outside consulting firm to work with us, to develop the strategic plan. It has allowed us to achieve longer-term objectives. Instead of worrying about a broken sewing machine, management has been able to think about associate training, better personal presentation. It doesn't matter who comes up with the idea, it's that we embrace it as a team."

When the chain was completely reacquired from Dylex in 1996, management crafted a "brand promise." As Larry describes it, "We're in the business of assisting men in developing a confident personal image, in all aspects of their life, any time, place, or occasion."

Ken Wong, associate professor of business and marketing strategy at Queen's School of Business, observes that the fashion industry is constantly under threat from quick knock-offs. Innovation is quickly replicated at lower costs, and it is not enough at the retail level on fashion's leading edge to sell uniqueness at a premium price. "Quality for the customer becomes less a question of what you sell than of how you sell it. When you get to price point at Rosen, it's the experience you're buying."

"We don't perceive ourselves as being in the clothing business," Larry explains. "We don't just sell suits and sport jackets. It's a relationship-based business. My business is to get to know you, to have you build a relationship with one of my highly trained associates. I want to be your clothier for life. The whole key to our business is loyal clients. I strongly believe we have a corporate culture that has a love of quality and a love of clients. And building customer relationships is a managed process."

Prioritizing customer satisfaction can yield savings in human resources. People generally don't like to serve unhappy customers, or work for a company with customer-related problems that are not necessarily of their own making. Staff turnover can be high because of worker dissatisfaction; even the number of sick days can increase. Having to constantly recruit new staff and deal with absenteeism generates a host of costs, and staffing problems tend to create a vicious feedback loop of compounding crises: more staff turnover (and a steady reduction in the quality of staff, as recruiting top candidates becomes more difficult) creates more unhappy customers, which in turn fuels discontent in staff ranks.

And not prioritizing customer satisfaction can cause an enterprise to completely misread the approach required to address revenue problems. If the reason for a decline in sales is poor staff training, no amount of advertising spending or price cuts will effectively mend the problem.

At Harry Rosen, it was recognized that even motivated, highly skilled, and highly trained salespeople could not cultivate a strong clientele without support. The founder had long been a font of sales wisdom, both a great student of customer behaviour and a teacher of winning sales techniques. But more was needed as the company resolved to retool itself for the modern retailing world.

The days have long passed when any enterprise larger than a modest storefront operation can effectively track customer spending and behaviour and provide targeted service to valued clients without the aid of technology. Customer relationship management (CRM) software often harnesses information that already exists within an enterprise but which is scattered through different departments—accounting, sales, marketing, customer service—with no way to create a coherent picture of performance from any number of angles: the identification of key customers; the performance of particular products and services not only in terms of raw dollar performance but according to identifiable customers and market subsegments; and the relationship (or not) between marketing initiatives and downstream sales, to name just a few valuable snapshots.

Customer relationship management aims to reach beyond the basic details of how a particular product or service is performing on the basis of fundamental metrics like revenue, profit, and inventory turnover, and instead understand the dynamics of the relationship between the customer and the enterprise. A business needs to know not only how much it is selling of what to whom, but if it is selling the right things to the right customers. It needs to know if the business is standing still while the market is moving in a new direction; if it is becoming a haven for a particular product or service with limited growth potential, while larger opportunities are being left to competitors to address. It needs to know if its customer base is experiencing necessary renewal, or if the company has become married to a particular aging demographic, with dwindling revenue potential. It needs, above all, to fully understand its target market. There hasn't been one identified yet that doesn't have some amount of segmentation. Those segments must be identified, their particular needs (and relative spending) assessed, and products or services—as well as marketing and customer-service strategies—created for them. The enterprise must know if its brand identification is flexible enough to function across all target markets, or if distinct brand identification strategies need to be shaped for these separate markets.

But when all is said and done, sales happen one customer at a time. Harry Rosen understood this when he founded his one-store empire in 1954, and that bald fact permeates the modern retail organization of sixteen stores with $160 million in sales—one customer, one transaction. Then do it again, and again. Make them want to come back. And make sure you understand them as best you can.

"The Harry Rosen story is one I can very much relate to," says Ken Wong. "When I was an MBA student, I helped start up a music store. When we began, we were a thousand square feet, and were up against major retailers. We went around to music teachers, to professional musicians, asking them things like, what kind of reeds do you use? We'd keep index cards on what reeds a professional musician used, when they were going to come in, and stock accordingly.

"Index cards are the most basic form of CRM. The Harry Rosen chain is using technology the way it's supposed to be used, by creating an electronic concierge. What the company has been able to do is take what Larry Rosen's father used to do personally for a much smaller client base and use technology to do the same thing for a much larger one."

Exactly how the company has been able to do it can be seen at a sales station on the third floor of the flagship Harry Rosen store in Toronto. An associate logs into the chain's CRM software, SalesLogix. A window pops up, telling him that he has a list of overdue activities: three to-do's, twenty-four telephone calls to return, and four meetings to attend. There's another window telling him he has sixteen clients with recent purchases who require a follow-up "satisfaction call." It's just the tip of the iceberg in the chain's CRM implementation. CRM is so fundamental to the Harry Rosen of today that it is impossible to imagine the chain operating without it.

"The big difference with us is in how we use CRM," says Larry. "We don't use it as a marketing gimmick. We will mine it for data—if we're doing a made-to-measure mailing, we'll choose the appropriate customers from the database. But what we do differently is we take CRM to the front line with our associates."

In many CRM implementations, companies forget what the "RM" stands for: relationship management—not *data* management. Any process that makes the management of a relationship impersonal doesn't have a bona fide relationship at its core. When it is done poorly, CRM is just a back-office tool, a way to manage accounts and inventory, to extract data on customer activities that might be useful in marketing and advertising decisions but leaves the individual customer unrecognized and unappreciated. A stream of numbers reduces the customer to being just another number, another end-product of a spreadsheet calculation. "People want a positive relationship," Larry explains. "They don't want to be a number. It's not rocket science. The rocket science is in executing the strategy."

The CRM strategy at Harry Rosen succeeds because it stitches together several crucial factors of the high-end clothing retail business. For starters, sales associates can be successful only if they develop a trusted and valued relationship with a client. It's not about making one sport jacket sale, but about turning a walk-in customer into somebody who looks to Harry Rosen for a wide range of clothing, from casual to formal, for years. "Our philosophy is simple," says Larry. "Men basically are reluctant shoppers. We need to develop a positive relationship with them. When you do, they can be almost a lifetime annuity."

"It's not looking to answer esoteric questions with CRM," says Wong of the Harry Rosen chain. "It's asking how much someone's business is worth over that person's lifetime. Other companies are doing this by the seat of their pants and hoping the results come through. What Harry Rosen is doing is institutionalizing what comes naturally to the classic entrepreneur, but doesn't come naturally to the general population.

"There's a great message for all companies. Ask people what Harry Rosen is known for, and the last thing will be CRM. For

Harry Rosen, it's not about the specific technology. It's about managing the specific information in the most effective way."

For associates and the chain overall to be successful, associates need to develop their own client list. "You can earn a good living," says Larry of the associates, noting that the chain currently has fifteen who generate $1 million each in retail spending annually. That's almost 10 percent of revenues from the dedication of fifteen front-line people. "We're the prestige employer of the industry. If you're interested in men's fashion, we're the game. We have tremendous training. We don't just throw you to the wolves. We spend $1 million a year on training, which is uncanny for our size. Our turnover in associates is very low, and gets very, very low once someone has been with us for three years and has built a client base."

The challenge is managing that client base intelligently, once you have it. "People in sales are naturally gregarious," Larry explains, "but your memory only allows you to remember your top fifteen customers. How do you develop a relationship with the customers between sixteen and a hundred?" Some associates can cite a personal customer base of more than two hundred people. It's impossible to keep track of them all without help.

In the old days, that help took the form of index cards containing basic information about the customer. Now, CRM software does the job, and in a way that makes an associate a much more productive employee while at the same time delivering a higher standard of service. Associates know their customers like never before.

While there can be something almost Orwellian about the level of detail that a CRM database can contain and interpret about a business's customers, CRM software works to the benefit of the customer and business alike if it's deployed in enhancing "RM." A top Harry Rosen customer (we'll call him Mr. Jones) is called up in SalesLogix. He's a forty-nine-year-old president of an investment firm, and his file contains the expected contact details (including the preferred contact method), along with some personal information that can jog a salesperson's memory: the names of his wife and kids, for example. The typical database file will also contain personal notes about where a customer vacationed, which, beyond providing a subject of small talk, tells the associate important things about clothing needs—a golf holiday in the Carolinas every February points toward a need for casual wear, and when that need is to be purchased. There's also a record of the man's fit requirements—in this case, that Mr. Jones wears a 44R to 46R, that his neck measurement is 16 1/12, among other dimensions. If Mr. Jones prefers side vents, that will be taken note of as well.

Mr. Jones is one of the chain's best clients. His file shows that he has, since 1995, spent more than $80,000 at Harry Rosen. The system also tracks at which stores he has done his spending. And, crucially in Mr. Jones's case, it shows *when* he does that spending. Larry smiles at the data: Mr. Jones is a personal friend. "He's a binge shopper." The system shows that he spent $15,000 on twenty-nine items on April 9. His historic spending profile tells a consistent story. Mr. Jones shops in the spring, in April or May, and does the vast majority of his spending during one visit. Knowing this is not being nosy. It's being customer attentive. Once a year, Mr. Jones is prepared to spend a substantial amount of money in a single visit to a Harry Rosen store. His associate needs to be keenly attuned to this. An appointment must be arranged that is convenient to Mr. Jones. The associate must be ready with the right clothing options to make the most of Mr. Jones's time, and to make the shopping experience enjoyable for him.

"The Harry Rosen chain doesn't just understand how the customer defines quality," says Wong. "It understands how the customer acts around its product. This business understands what the customer does when he shops, and makes it very easy for him to shop the way he wants to. It really is the essence of putting yourself in the customer's head and seeing the world through his eyes."

The CRM database can be accessed from numerous viewpoints, and one of them is by clothing line. Zegna suits (along with Zegna Sport) are a popular line at Harry Rosen, and a search of the top customers of Zegna reveals that Mr. Jones is among them. In fact, he buys nothing but Zegna for his suit needs. If a new shipment of Zegna arrives, Mr. Jones will be one of the customers personally notified.

"The use of the system is not random," says Larry. "Associates are required to keep in contact with their clients. We'll take away a client if they don't keep in touch with him at least once a season. A manager can also use it to keep track of how many people an associate hasn't been in touch with."

It's possible for an enterprise to be *too* customer focused, too dedicated to servicing the needs of its customer base. The hazard comes in not appreciating that maintaining unswerving loyalty to a particular set of customers, who delivered prosperity at a particular point in time, can mean being allied to the particular needs of one demographic group, and following that group up the population curve over time. A company can start out with a clientele of thirtysomethings, and through unwavering devotion to that customer set, find itself servicing fiftysomethings in twenty years, having along the way lost touch with products and services of prime interest to the thirty- and fortysomethings.

That's not to say it's a bad idea to cater to fiftysomethings, and in some industries it would be foolhardy not to try to keep pace with the requirements of an aging customer base. When the recreational marine industry began growing in earnest through fibreglass production in the 1970s, boat builders generally followed their customers up the market, as they showed the desire (and the increasing ability to spend) to trade up to ever larger, ever more expensive yachts. New models were added at the top end, but some builders ultimately suffered when they were unable to maintain production models at the lower end. Their original customers were selling their well-maintained, second-hand boats (which, if well built to begin with, had a long life ahead of them) to the next generation of entry-level customers. The resale market suffocated the new-boat market at the smaller end of the product lines. Production costs and a lack of product innovation meant that some builders were unable to offer any new models less than thirty feet long that could compete with the second-hand market. They were undermined by their original successes, and distracted by the appeal of making high-margin, high-dollar-value sales to the customers they started out with.

These builders could take some consolation in the fact that, while they couldn't figure out how to build a thirty-foot boat that would retail for less than $100,000, the customers they were growing old with were at least prepared to buy a forty-foot boat for $250,000. But in high-end menswear retailing, there is no such benefit to following an aging customer through his buying cycle.

Older consumers are right to protest against ageism in consumer product marketing, and companies in general ignore them at their peril. But for a retailing operation like Harry Rosen, which aims at consumers between the ages of twenty-five and fifty-five, it is well understood that the average age of its customer base cannot be permitted to increase over time. If it does, it means that crucial customers in the twenty- and thirtysomething ranges are not coming aboard. Without those new customers, who can be developed into valued clients with years of spending ahead of them, the company faces a precipitous drop in revenues as the present set of clients moves through their fifties. Those aging clients hopefully will continue to shop at Harry Rosen, and the store will be delighted to service them (and many do transfer their clothing spending habits from business to casual wear), but it is a cold, hard fact of menswear retailing that when men enter their fifties, their spending on clothing often plummets.

"A man over fifty-five buys very little clothing," observes Larry. "A man at forty spends a lot, because he's at the peak of his career."

Generally, the fiftysomething customers have done the better part of their corporate ladder climbing, and may even be taking early retirement. They just don't feel a recurring need to have the latest power suit. Even casual wear demands can drop as their social networking (often tied to business) tapers off.

"Our strategic goal is to keep our average customer age at thirty-eight," says Larry. "With the baby boomers now between thirty-nine and fifty-nine, it's easy to concentrate on them, but it's a bad strategy. We have to make sure our marketing is aiming younger." The design of the Toronto flagship store, for example, is organized not so much according to formal versus casual but according to demographic targets. One floor is aimed at the twenty-five- to forty-year-old set. Another one takes aim at thirty-five to fifty. "We carry Hugo Boss, Versace, Ted Baker ... The younger man today wears a slimmer suit, a plain front trouser. Probably half of the suits we sell are 'fashion suits.'"

The company takes its sales research seriously. Recently, customer surveying in one of its cities revealed an age average of forty-three. "Alarms went off," says Larry. "We decided to change our marketing there. You have to be always renewing yourself."

It's a truism that a market, and an enterprise's roll call of customers, are not one and the same thing. They are distinct entities, but the relationship between them is fluid. The dimensions and characteristics of a market ideally dictate how an enterprise identifies opportunity and then goes about servicing that market. The enterprise measures and monitors its customer base to determine how well it is achieving the goal of meeting that target market's needs. As the market's characteristics evolve, the enterprise must be attuned, and moving with it accordingly.

But a market is not a static object of study. Needs and wants, while understood to be different things, are both pliable. Another truism: People don't know what they want until they're told they want it, and people don't know that their wants actually are needs until they're also told this is the case. Enterprises, in identifying, cultivating, and retaining customers, must not only identify demands, they must create them as well. The market to a significant degree is a creation of marketing. And customers must hear a persuasive marketing message, collectively as well as individually.

The Harry Rosen chain understands that competition has two dimensions. Most obviously, there are the competing menswear operations—not only in the city markets of their individual stores, but globally. "Our customer tends to be a sophisticated travelling customer," Larry notes. "He can buy when he's in New York City. We have to be aligned with what's going on in the world, and be as current as London and New York stores." But Larry also understands that he is competing with other discretionary expenditures. The competition for a man's clothing budget in the larger picture is not the tailor down the road but a hot tub, or a ski vacation at Whistler, or a home theatre system. "You don't *need* that leather jacket or cashmere sweater," Larry observes. And even when you have bought a suit from him, as a business wear necessity, in terms of wear and tear, you're probably good for ten years. "You don't have to replace a great suit," Larry notes. But if you appreciate style, you will want to.

Truth be told, most things that people own don't fall into the category of necessary. Consumers have a bewildering array of options for their discretionary spending. And within those options are a bewildering array of choice in price point and sophistication. The total discretionary budget may be finite, but the flexibility in portioning it out is considerable. Simply studying the marketplace to determine potential revenues will not yield the answers that create a viable business plan. Demographics are crucial to determining where a Harry Rosen store can be located, but demand then must be created. The demand is created by fostering relationships with customers, by understanding who they are, how clothing does and can fit into their lifestyle.

Not everyone can be turned into a fashion enthusiast. But many can be made at least to appreciate the importance of quality clothing, from casual to formal, and, most importantly, to appreciate that Harry Rosen makes the experience of maintaining a wardrobe not only painless but even pleasant. "A relationship," Larry puts it simply, "means they have fun when they buy, and they spend more money. We're the kings of relationship building. We're advisors, not sellers. It doesn't matter if you're a clothes horse or a utilitarian shopper. An experienced associate should be able to read you properly and lead you."

The Harry Rosen chain has been successful by taking the long view on customer relationships: of prioritizing turning the customers into the highly valued clients who will come to the store to be dressed (as opposed to buying items piecemeal) for all occasions, and do so for years. The importance of customer satisfaction to cultivating and retaining clients was instilled by the founder long before any CRM software appeared on the premises.

"We've had the greatest role model in the world: my father," says Larry. "He'll break off a meeting to deal with a client. He'll go to their house if he has to." A key operating principle is that the client is always right. "We don't accept an unhappy client. You can't build your client satisfaction principles around the half percent that take advantage of you. You have to make sure that your client recovery strategy is very aggressive. Our clients are successful. A guy who is forty years old and is going to spend $3000 to $5000 every year has a net present value for us of $75,000. If that guy's unhappy with something he purchased from us—even if he shouldn't have thrown the shirt in the washing machine with bleach—I've got to make him happy. I'm not thinking about a $100 shirt. I'm thinking about the $75,000 he will spend with us as a lifetime customer. We've done some ridiculous things for people, but when you do something extraordinary, they tell everybody, and you can't pay for that kind of advertising.

"If you exceed expectations," Larry Rosen emphasizes, "it makes people fans of you."

The Deloitte perspective

Building and sustaining a customer-focused approach to sales and marketing

Harry Rosen, a retailer of some of the most powerful brands in quality menswear, has built itself into a powerful national brand. That brand is based not simply on what it sells—because styles and designers change and fall in and out of fashion—but in how it sells. The brand provides a service promise to its customers, and this promise has been used effectively as a marketing and sales strategy to communicate the company's value proposition. The chain's absolute commitment to its customer in service and satisfaction is made possible by an internal commitment to employ highly trained sales associates, and to ensure that those associates know individual customers with database precision. Harry Rosen doesn't just hire salespeople to sell the clothing it stocks and tailors. It provides those salespeople with constant training and a customer relationship management system that aids them in achieving sales goals while maximizing the customer experience.

The Rosen management team has had to be quick to keep up to date with changes affecting their target markets. Execution is not fly-by-night or trial and error but is based on the Rosen philosophy to invest in resources such as communication, technology, training, and personnel to increase customers from the identified target segments. Using excellent customer profiling technology, management is able to identify indications of market shifts, emerging trends, or new opportunities, and to plan marketing and sales strategies that are aligned with customer behaviours. If successful, a company like this is in a win-win-win situation: fewer customer complaints and returns turn customer satisfaction into brand loyalty; employee morale increases, as customer satisfaction correlates well with employee morale; and corporate results improve.

The Harry Rosen story demonstrates key lessons for companies trying to build this type of organization:

- From its beginning as a single tailor's shop, Harry Rosen has listened to customers. Clothing is a personal choice, and people define themselves by the clothes they wear. Listening to customers allows the retailer to satisfy their needs and identify the buyer-specific sales opportunities.
- Harry Rosen has been able to anticipate the needs of its customers and provide well-appointed clothing, whether for the office, a social occasion, or the cottage.
- A customer is more than a single sale. Harry Rosen strives to develop a lifetime relationship, placing customer service in the context of the future value (or net present value) of that relationship.
- The enterprise must identify and remain current with changes affecting its target market, anticipate new customer segments, and discard unprofitable segments.

In optimizing customer service and target-market opportunities, a business should:

- Segment the target market to identify particular needs and develop new products and services if there is a gap in the current product and service portfolio.
- Build brand differentiation strategies to best cater to the different market segments. Communicate regularly and consistently the brand meaning that most benefits each segment.
- Invest in resources such as communication, technology, personnel, and training to increase individual customers' average transaction amount and frequency of repurchase.
- Establish effective communication processes throughout the organization to disseminate customer information and to collect customer feedback.

6 Moving in all the right directions

Developing and leveraging core competencies

Armour Transportation Systems

Canada's 50 Best Managed Companies winner, 2003 and 2004

In the early 1930s, Gordon Armour developed a side interest in the transportation business, with a solitary truck operating out of Taylor Village, New Brunswick. He hauled hay, as well as gravel, from the small farming community to nearby Moncton. Those staples kept Armour going through the Depression and the war years. As his delivery range expanded, he discovered backhaul. After hauling hay to Nova Scotia, he would return with apples from the Annapolis Valley. Soap and chocolate also made trips back home. After the war, Armour began handling other merchandise, including Christmas trees, which he drove to the United States. The business was a full-time concern by 1954, and in the 1960s, there was an active little trucking company, with about a dozen trucks and a dozen employees, for the most part hauling foodstuffs and soft drinks out of the Acadian town of Dieppe.

But after thirty years in the trucking business, Gordon Armour wanted out. His son, Wesley, wanted to keep the company going and so offered to take it over. It was 1967. There was no real money in it. Were it not for the teaching job of his wife, Patricia, Wesley Armour might have starved.

"It was a ten-vehicle business, a one-man show," Wesley recalls. "I was driver, accountant, and president. The decisions I made with ten trucks were more critical because it was a matter of survival. I was twenty-two years old, living on my wife's salary, trying to give direction to employees twice my age. Now, I have extremely good people, and can afford to make a few mistakes without destroying the company."

Not that there have been many mistakes. Armour Transportation Systems is a diversified company with fifteen hundred employees, headquartered in Moncton. A major player in shipping in Atlantic Canada, it is active throughout North America through its own operations and alliances. Trucks are still at the heart of the business, but it can no longer be described as a "trucking company." It owns a courier, and a warehousing operation, and its IT systems are so sophisticated that some of its freight customers have signed on as clients rather than bothering to develop their own IT infrastructure. Under Wesley's direction, the simple trucking fleet of Dieppe, while remaining a family-owned enterprise, has turned into an award-winning transportation company. In doing so, it has thrived in a deregulated trucking environment that crushed many competitors.

How? By recognizing what it did best, could do best, and needed to do best.

Trucking in North America has undergone a painful, if ultimately necessary, transformation since Wesley acquired his father's modest operation. The North American industry was highly regulated in terms of who could participate and what they could charge, and even the routes on which they could operate. Inflexibility in shipping costs distorted the economic infrastructure. It caused manufacturers to place their factories closer to the markets for their finished goods rather than the sources of their raw materials. Once the deregulation movement gathered steam in the United States in the 1970s, Canada was inevitably obliged to follow.

The American trucking industry fell under the regulatory blanket with the Motor Traffic Act of 1935, which placed highway transportation under the jurisdiction of the Interstate Commerce Commission (ICC). (Rail traffic had been heavily regulated by Washington since the Interstate Commerce Act went into effect in 1887.) The ICC controlled entry into and exit from the interstate trucking industry, the routes that companies could use, and the rates they charged, and the teamsters' union brought its own oversight to bear. By the 1970s it was clear that the U.S. economy needed relief from the costs produced by transportation regulation. The ICC began to loosen entry limitations in the late 1970s, and in 1980 the Motor Carrier Act, while not completely deregulating the trucking industry, encouraged a veritable swarm of new participants. With the ICC's replacement by the Surface Transportation Board of the Department of Transportation in 1995, trucking became fully deregulated. Rates and routes were liberated, while safety and operations continued to be overseen.

Interstate carriers in the United States soared from eighteen thousand in 1980 to about fifty thousand by the turn of the millennium. And Canadian trucking companies could see deregulation coming their way like an eighteen-wheeler on a prairie horizon. The Canadian industry had been as heavily regulated as its interstate cousins, although in a different way. Trucking was controlled by provinces, and interprovincial carriers had to jump through the requisite regulatory hoops of each province in which they aspired to operate—provided they could get permission to operate. Rates were as controlled in Canada as they had been in the United States, and there was no overarching federal regulation.

The prospect of deregulation was, frankly, frightening to the established carriers. It would usher in new competition and new ways of doing business. And if the American experience was anything to go on, the transition would have a rash of problems related to the newcomers. But there was no stopping it. The passage of the federal Motor Vehicle Transport Act in 1987 ushered in the new era of deregulation north of the border. The U.S.–Canada Free Trade Agreement then went into effect on January 1, 1989, and its successor, the North American Free Trade Agreement (NAFTA) of 1994, required a harmonization in transportation regulations between Canada, the United States, and Mexico by 2000. Further deregulation came with the 1995 Agreement on Internal Trade, under which Ottawa and the provinces agreed to dismantle interprovincial barriers.

The established Canadian trucking firms resisted the regulatory dismantling, but it happened regardless—and, as predicted, with much trauma. As new small- and medium-sized carriers entered the market, business became do-or-die. David Bradley, CEO of the Canadian Trucking Alliance, has described this first phase of Canadian deregulation as having been marked by "blood-thirsty competition, increased service demand, downward pressure on freight rates and depressed driver pay." As rates fell and competition ratcheted up, companies failed, and many truckers who weren't seeing their wages decline were losing their jobs altogether.

"The new entries didn't know the costs, and financing was easy for them to get," says Wesley. "I sort of blame the financial institutions. Many if not most of the older companies couldn't deal with the new environment. The only ones that seemed to survive were family-owned businesses."

Fortunately, Armour Transportation was one of them. As he expanded the company he'd acquired from his father, Wesley recognized the advantages of being a family operation. He didn't have any shareholders or other investors to keep happy with profit payouts. He could reinvest whatever he made in the company, paying down buildings and vehicles. He had relocated the operation to Moncton Industrial Park, investing in vehicles, warehousing, office facilities, and a garage. "Rates were cutthroat, with little or no increase," he says of the introduction of deregulation. "We had to keep a very close eye on the bottom line and operate an extremely efficient company, because we couldn't get the pricing we needed. During that time, I was able to get myself debt free, and put the company in a strong equity position. We're still that way today. If the economy went south in the next few years, the company could survive well."

Wesley had served as president of the Canadian Trucking Alliance (CTA) in the 1980s, when deregulation was thundering in from the not-so-distant horizon, and the CTA membership was adamantly opposed to it. "Today, I'd say I'd probably want to see deregulation," Wesley volunteers. "Once it came, I decided from day one not to fight it. I said to my managers, 'We're in a new environment, with lots of opportunities to expand. Let's jump on them.'"

It's not always easy for a company to recognize its core competencies—or even to recognize what business it is actually in. Process can be mistaken for the actual service. This was particularly true of trucking, because it had been sheltered by government regulation and companies had their existence defined by the parameters of those regulations. They moved goods on public highways, inside trucks. They were about a particular kind of machinery serving a particular role in the economy that had been considered so fundamental to its overall well-being that legislators for decades had chosen to place the industry in a straitjacket of approved rates and licensed participants. When the straitjacket came off, many established companies didn't know what business they were in. And many new companies didn't know what business they were getting into. They thought they were still filling the backs of trucks with watermelons and machine tools, only now having to do it in a climate of merciless, rate-slashing competition.

Which, to some degree, was true, in that it was still the trucking business. It remained a vital component of the economy, albeit one in which competition was unprecedentedly tight. But survival was going to depend on seeing beyond the rigs and panel trucks and recognizing exactly what it was Armour was doing, and how the company could do it in a different and better way.

"When business became cutthroat," says Wesley, "I said to my managers, 'What is our future here?' I decided that we had to be more than a trucker. We had to be a total supplier of transportation."

That didn't mean Armour was going to start investing in aircraft and ships. Rather, it meant that Armour had to understand the services that customers required, and how to provide them, better than anyone else in their niche.

"What I think is really interesting about Armour, and it's valid for many companies, is that it defined the customer problem to be solved in the right way," says Elspeth Murray, associate professor of strategy and new ventures at Queen's School of Business.

"Armour's business really wasn't about moving stuff from point A to point B. It was about solving the logistical issues for the customers. They were able to say, 'If we're going to solve the logistics problems for our customers in the future, we'd better have a set of capabilities, collectively known as a core competence, so that we can respond to whatever their changing needs are better than anybody else.'"

"For most companies," Wesley says, speaking with an abundance of experience, "transportation is a pain in the butt. They just want to get product out the door and into the customer's hands." Companies, in other words, get into the shipping business themselves only when they have to, and stay in it only when they think they have to. It's a complication of operations that business people generally wish didn't exist, and they will gladly hand it off to a third party if they hear the right value proposition: no worries, cost effective. One of Armour Transportation's core competencies was removing the ache in managerial backsides. Armour's trucks were part of the pain relief, but ultimately not the solution in and of themselves. For one thing, every truck needs a driver, and the driver's typical role in the industry was desperate for a hundred-thousand-kilometre overhaul when deregulation began.

It is fair to say that, before deregulation, the average driver in the trucking industry was little more than a heavy equipment operator, someone who piloted a vehicle from A to B. The drivers' fundamental skill set was considered to be in the area of clutching, safe driving, and keeping to a schedule. In 1988, only 6 percent of truck drivers employed by licensed carriers had a post-secondary education—a university degree or college diploma, or some apprenticeship training or a trades certificate. Despite the romance of country-and-western hurtin' songs, truck driving did not have broad appeal to the available pool of the employable. It was dominated by white males, and newcomers were typically single and in their late twenties, able to tolerate long working hours alone at the wheel, especially in the case of long-haul drivers. When deregulation injected stiff competition to the industry, trucking companies were caught in labour crises that were, in some cases, of their own making. Relying on a pool of single white men for recruitment already severely limited hiring possibilities. An already challenging job was made less appealing when vicious competition suppressed driver wages—labour costs inevitably having to buckle under to market forces. Then the entire industry, along with the rest of the economy, drove into the murk of the early 1990s recession.

Unemployment among truck drivers reached 16 percent in 1991. When trucking business rebounded with the strong recovery that began in 1994, companies faced a serious shortage of drivers. Those who hadn't given up the profession—discouraged by layoffs or diminishing pay envelopes, and weary of long hours, the stress of driving, and separation from family once they married and began raising children—often lacked the skills the new economy and heightened competition required.

The industry overall needed to deliver more than just the customer's goods. It had to deliver a competitive edge based on more than raw cost. Otherwise, transportation companies were in a losing bidding war to deliver services that had become mere commodities, trapped in a downward spiral of cost-cutting to deliver price reductions.

Customers themselves drove some of the requisite changes. Their own heightened competitive circumstances had led them to embrace cost-reduction strategies such as just-in-time inventory management; that particular strategy led to the shipping-and-receiving door. Trucking and other transportation firms had to rise to the challenge of precise tracking and delivery. Drivers had to become savvy in managing onboard computers and other electronic devices. Shipping was becoming internet-enabled. Global positioning systems were being employed to monitor fleets. These required skill sets that drivers hadn't needed to have before.

Beyond the issue of their being able to manage the new gizmos, drivers were a transportation company's front-line workers. More than half of a typical trucking company's employees are behind the wheel. They are the contact point with the customer, and in the post-deregulation market, drivers became crucial to winning and retaining customers. Salespeople could make all the promises they liked on price and delivery schedules and reliability, but ultimately the quality of service, and the value attached to it by the customer, came down to whoever was at the wheel. The driver, to such a tremendous degree, became the value proposition that differentiated between companies and allowed a transportation company to avoid the downward drift into a commodity pricing war.

Like other trucking operations, Armour has had to contend with a persistent shortage of drivers. But the company has managed to avoid a serious problem by hanging on to its drivers. It has done so by recognizing their importance to the company's success and therefore ensuring low turnover, and so building relationships through them between the company and customers. Armour Transportation certainly has salespeople, and they are important and productive, but Wesley recognizes that many sales, many new leads, and the retention of many accounts take place at the interface between the driver and the "guy at the back door" of the customer's premises. "I'll hear, 'Don't ever take Joe away from this run.' I make sure I thank Joe for what he's done. And we get a lot of leads from our drivers."

Companies that are successful in defining and leveraging core competencies "have to have a certain type of leadership and leadership style," says Murray. "The essence of core competence is that you have a set of skills and capabilities that collectively are hard for competitors to copy. And the most difficult capabilities to copy are related to people."

Wesley considers every one of his company's fifteen hundred employees to be in sales. Not only actual salespeople, of course, and the above-mentioned drivers, but also dispatch workers and customer service staff. They are people who come to the company, and stay, and build invaluable relationships with the customers. "We have a skilled and trained staff. Our employee turnover is significantly lower than the industry average. Our low driver turnover is almost unheard of."

In 2004, Georges Leblanc of Moncton was named the Canadian Trucking Alliance/Volvo Trucks Canada National Driver of the Year. In his thirty-three years of driving, all of them with Armour, Leblanc had logged 5.2 million collision-free kilometres. "Georges is exactly what we want in our industry for the perfect highway professional operator," Wesley Armour said when the award was announced. "He is extremely good at his job, smart, has a positive attitude, very caring for others, excellent with customers, an outstanding safe driver, understands all safety and highway regulations and complies with them without being managed. Most of all, he is just an outstanding individual."

Far less publicly recognized are the efforts Armour employees make, day in, day out, to keep customers happy. When Hurricane Juan ravaged Halifax in October 2003, right before Thanksgiving, Armour staff were instrumental in getting ample stock not only quickly back onto shelves at Loblaws outlets, but in time for stores to open for Sunday Thanksgiving shopping. "Had it not been for the contribution and efforts of your team," Mark Butler, vice-president, Superstore operations, emailed Armour staffers, "the stores would not have been able to open in the condition which they did.... Although you probably all think you are just doing your job, I really feel you went over and above your regular call of duty." Not surprisingly, in four years, Armour has significantly increased the business it does with Loblaws in Atlantic Canada.

Another unpublicized case in point: In October 2002, Michael Walton, director of sales at the Fredericton office of Lantic Sugar, received a call from Lantic's quality control department in Montreal. It needed a sugar sample gathered from a remote Nova Scotia location, now. It was 4:30 on a Friday afternoon. Walton was facing a round-trip of ten to twelve hours by car through the night to retrieve and deliver it himself, and even at that, the sample would still not reach Montreal until Saturday. He called Larry Tower, vice-president of operations at Armour, looking for help. Minutes later, Tower had Bob Briggs, then manager of special projects, on the way to collect the sample. The Armour people had it in Montreal by 8:15 that same evening, less than four hours after Walton placed the call to Tower. Walton was so astonished by the service that he wrote a letter of appreciation to Wesley.

As deregulation pressed hard on his business, Wesley had to think strategically about what that business was, and how to make the most of his competitive advantages. He operated a fleet of trucks, but he was really in the transportation services business. What he could offer customers was not simply a driver and vehicle to haul something from one location to another but an infrastructure solution to their shipping needs. He recognized that he had certain scale advantages in Atlantic Canada. The region had a lot of terrain without a whole lot of people—only about 2.6 million. Companies operating in the region faced burdens in managing transportation and inventory efficiently that might not exist in a major centre such as Vancouver or Toronto. Armour began to find opportunities to become what was essentially an outside supplier of inside services.

Some of those opportunities came from the company's investment in IT systems. Armour's IT infrastructure was so good that customers found that it made more sense to sign on as a client rather than go to the expense and bother of upgrading themselves. Other opportunities lay in convincing companies to outsource some or all of their transportation operations to Armour.

The company made this possible by investing significantly in warehousing, creating Armour Logistics Services (ALS). With a recent expansion, Armour can offer over five hundred thousand square feet of warehousing space in Moncton, the transportation hub of Atlantic Canada. It has another fifty thousand square feet in Dartmouth, Nova Scotia, and, through a partnership with the industrial warehousing company Cargocan Logistics, forty-four thousand square feet in St. John's, Newfoundland. And it's not just a matter of offering empty space in large buildings. The company employs a customized warehouse software package, called ALS/2000. It includes an electronic order desk for processing and shipping customer orders for the client, computerized inventory tracking, and accounts receivable support.

In some contract arrangements, all the customer's warehousing, transportation, and inventory management and ordering functions are handled by Armour. The operation can be so seamless that even the truck drivers, who are employed by Armour, dress in the uniforms of the client. A showcase example for Armour is its relationship with the Pepsi Bottling Group, a subsidiary of Pepsi International, in Dartmouth. Since 2002,

Armour has handled the job of getting Pepsi product to market. Pepsi still employs their own delivery drivers, but Armour handles the rest. "We pick up its soft drinks off the end of the line, do its warehousing, pick orders, and load the Pepsi trucks in the night," says Wesley. Armour gets the Moosehead and Labatt beer brands to market with a similar arrangement. "Flexibility" comes up frequently in Wesley's discussion of his company's successes. "We have to be very flexible, and think outside the box. We've had to customize some of our services for our customers. Sometimes you might say, 'We already have systems in this company. How are we going to adapt to a customer's system and still maintain control?' We think we can do that, and just get our heads around it. If we're going to be a provider of transportation services and have growth and opportunities, we have to be flexible. If you're not flexible, you're limited in your business opportunities."

That said, Armour has focused on a particular, if broad, shipping niche. "We don't do gravel, used furniture, or logging. They're so different than what we do. Everything we do is around the general freight business. All the parts tie in well together, and because we're dealing a lot with the same accounts, that gives us a competitive advantage over somebody who is just a trucker."

In addition to investing in its own infrastructure, Armour has been able to grow through acquisitions (made easy by its ready access to capital) and alliances. "We've made a lot of acquisitions over the years," says Wesley. "Sometimes the goal was to expand the business in Atlantic Canada; at other times it was to put services into other parts of the country, or to add a new service, such as courier." Purchasing PoleStar in 1989 gave Armour long-haul capability throughout the NAFTA region. Acquiring a courier company in 2001 has given Armour Transportation a revenue generator that complements its general freight business. Armour

Courier Service (ACS) operates in Nova Scotia, New Brunswick, and Prince Edward Island, with same-day service available between Fredericton, Saint John, Moncton, and Bathurst, New Brunswick, and overnight to most addresses in the Maritimes. An alliance with FedEx extends ACS's service internationally. Intermodal service also led it into an alliance with CN.

Wesley became particularly aware of the importance of alliances while he was president of the Canadian Trucking Alliance. He took note of how U.S. trucking firms, which were already dealing with deregulation, found a competitive edge in the less-than-load (LTL) market. "The ones successful in the United States became dominant in a region and then formed partnerships in outside areas. We've done this with many U.S. and Canadian partners. A delivery from Moncton to Hawaii is seamless to our customers. We're responsible for the shipment all the way through."

"Armour is a great example of defying that put-down. 'You're just a little company on the east coast of Canada,'" says Murray. "The location doesn't mean you can't compete with the big boys. It comes down to strong leadership, getting the most out of your people, and being plugged into your customers, so that you can see a problem of theirs being solved in an entirely new way." And Murray sees a whole new set of problems for shipping customers awaiting solutions from an adaptable firm such as Armour. Deregulation had provided the first serious shock to the trucking industry. Now the post-9/11 environment is raising a host of logistical headaches in cross-border trade. "It needs to deal with issues such as proof of point of origin, of destination, all the customs issues," notes Murray. "For shippers, the competitive edge is coming from proving your logistics are good. The needs to service the customer are even higher than ever."

To Wesley Armour, core competencies at Armour are multifold. He offers the following:

On strong, disciplined leadership: "Managers are visible, and have constant contact with front lines. They're listening, learning, and communicating. And the CEO is the leader." Strategic issues are dealt with in an executive group, with the input of managers, with Wesley overseeing the process and giving direction. "I try to not make the decision. If you're always making a decision for people, they'll wait for you to make one. I try to let managers manage. If I don't like what they're suggesting, I'll ask questions. But you have to recognize that day-to-day decisions are made down in the trenches by the managers. Top managers in most companies don't make decisions that affect success on a day-to-day basis. Businesses can lose sight of this and think the top core of the executive are running the business. It's those at the next levels down who are deciding success and failure. I'm a strong believer in letting your managers manage, but that they must be accountable."

On exceptional customer relationships and relationship management: "The customer comes first. Everyone says it, but we believe it. We'll do whatever the customer wants—if they pay for it!"

On the sales force: "There's been no turnover in ten years. That builds a strong relationship with the customer. When visiting a customer, the salesperson goes in first—not me." And everyone who works at Armour is in sales in some way. Especially the drivers.

On the operations managers: "They are responsible for sales in their region, and customer service."

On a skilled and trained staff, with unusually low turnover: "On-the-job training is very important. We customize the training for departments. Improving knowledge, taking courses, allows people to do their jobs better, and it builds morale." The employees have also won their share of personal awards; for instance, a driver on the Oland/Labatt account was named its outstanding supplier of the year. "The award went to the driver, not to me. He looks after the liquid sweetener going into the brewery. With zero direction from us, he did customer service on his own. A strong relationship with employees builds mutual trust and respect. That's hard for competitors to match."

On being innovative: "We're always flexible, and willing to change. Innovation has gone far beyond trucks and warehousing. The people are innovative. They are quick to make and adapt decisions."

On good acquisitions and alliances: It's about more than expanding the operating sphere. Partnering with large international companies such as Reimer and FedEx also has benefited Armour in its pursuit of operational excellence. "We can share with them, and learn from them. Complying with their systems is good, because it's made us a better, more disciplined company. We've been very lucky that way. A lot of our business is through partnerships. If we just operated in Atlantic Canada, we would be half the size we are."

On a willingness to deal head-on with challenges to arrive at solutions: "Often the best solutions come from your own people. That requires strong leadership, and good people skills, to motivate them. A lot of companies have great people but don't know how to motivate them." Outside advice "can be a help, but it can also cost you employees if the advice isn't good." However, in succession planning, Wesley felt it was critical that he turn to outside experts to properly structure ownership and responsibility for the next generation. (Two sons, Angus and Ralston, hold senior positions.) "Too many family businesses don't deal with those issues until they happen. We brought in the best people I could find from around the country to deal with it. Failure of family businesses is extremely high, and I think many fail because of poor succession planning."

The Deloitte perspective

Developing and leveraging core competencies

Armour Transportation excels because it focuses on what its customers want now and what they will need in the future. Armour understands its core competencies and is not afraid to build on them to broaden its service offering to meet evolving customer needs.

Wesley Armour has created a culture where all employees strive to provide exceptional customer service by focusing on the customer's wants and needs first. These employees are passionate about what they do, and it shows. When you combine a passion for customer service with this company's warm family environment, it is not surprising that Armour is one of Canada's 50 Best Managed companies.

The Armour story demonstrates that to grow a business over the long term, a company needs to protect, leverage, and develop its core competencies and to consider what activities (and therefore resources) will add value to its service offering.

Focusing on core competencies does not necessarily mean giving up activities to focus on what you do best. Leveraging core competencies can mean expanding your service offering, based on your unique position in the market. In Armour's case, its strength in shipping allowed it to expand its service offering within the supply chain beyond physical haulage to the provision of logistics solutions. As Armour illustrates, a core competency may reside outside the main business. This is evident in the company's development as an IT provider for freight customers, an outgrowth of the strength it developed in its own IT infrastructure.

Developing and leveraging core competencies involves these key steps:

- Fully develop the company's business strategy and value proposition.
- Identify the main things at which the company must excel—the core competencies.
- Determine the critical success and failure factors of the company, and clearly map those items back to the company's business strategy.

These core competencies need to be developed in such a way that they produce competitive advantages. In the case of Armour, the development and leveraging of its acquisition and integration skills allowed it to create a competitive advantage in the Atlantic region, and through alliances extend service to its regional customer base seamlessly throughout North America.

It is important to recognize that existing core competencies may need to change as the business strategy evolves. Existing core competencies need to be protected and leveraged and new competencies developed. Companies need to be critical of those functions performed at its business. If they are not a core competency or tied to business strategy, they should be outsourced to reduce cost and risk.

7 Booming through the bust

Attracting capital and managing finances

Mediagrif Interactive Technologies

Canada's 50 Best Managed Companies winner, 2002 and 2003

Little more than a decade on, it's worth remembering not only how much has been changed by the internet, but how much about the internet itself has changed. It's not just a matter of bandwidth and software. When the idea of Mediagrif Interactive Technologies was struck upon in late 1995, the basic technology components of the internet revolution were well established—email, the World Wide Web, internet protocol programming. But the investment environment that would give rise to (in Alan Greenspan's cautionary words in a speech on December 6, 1996) the "irrational exuberance" of markets, particularly with technology stocks, was just emerging.

The website of Amazon.com went live in July 1995, not long before Netscape Communications' initial public offering debuted on the NASDAQ on August 9, 1995, an event that is generally credited as breathing the first breath into the dot.com bubble. (Netscape had been formed in April 1994 to create a commercial version of the Mosaic web browser, and released the first edition of its browser in October 1994. In 1997, America Online paid enough for the start-up to have to account for $9 billion in goodwill.) There were other landmark events in the internet/communications world that year. Microsoft released its first browser, Explorer, in the fall, as part of Windows 95. And on September 20, AT&T, under pressure from the U.S. Justice Department's persistent antitrust investigations, announced it was breaking itself up into three separate companies, one of which was the former R&D department of Bell Labs, now to be known as Lucent Technologies.

Montreal's Mediagrif was poised on the initial surge of the internet wave, rather than riding its crest, as its business plan was quietly assembled in late 1995. The company was incorporated in February 1996—at virtually the same time U.S. president Bill Clinton was signing into law the Telecom Act, which aggressively disbanded cross-ownership restrictions in local and long-distance telephone markets and the cable industry, a move which proved to be key to the imminent explosion in investment activity. But the scale of the coming wave was not entirely recognized, particularly in Canada. Nortel Networks, Canada's telecommunications technology leader, was a latecomer to embracing the internet, having unveiled the Rapport Dialup Switch, its first unequivocal internet product, in 1995, and the company wouldn't make a strong shift away from its preferred networking vision and truly join the internet revolution until 1997. In venturing into the internet world fundamentally ahead of a networking giant like Nortel, the principals of Mediagrif were like a couple of fellows in a rowboat planting their bow in a Caribbean beach a week ahead of Columbus in the *Santa Maria*.

Which didn't necessarily make their task of launching a start-up in the business-to-business internet sector any easier. Head starts are always a good thing in areas of new technology, but Mediagrif and its technology were new enough, and early enough in the internet boom, to make raising investment capital a challenge. Money was not raining from the sky when Mediagrif started up, and the company would wait four years before moving forward with an initial public offering (IPO) of its own—waiting so long, in fact, that it was almost too late, as the entire dot.com boom was shifting into bust mode. But that Mediagrif was able to wait four years is indication enough that it did not represent the typical dot.com start-up, the archetypal form of which was a couple of university students holed up in a basement, writing killer code for an application without obvious market, fuelled by hundreds of thousands of dollars provided by a venture cap fund ... and then going public with a multimillion-dollar IPO without a foreseeable date on which revenues, never mind profits, would begin arriving.

Things, as investors have noticed, have changed in the worlds of tech start-ups and IPOs. But things were always very different for Mediagrif. For one thing, the start-up was seeded by love money. And only one of them actually had any money. For another thing, Mediagrif grew through the most irrationally exuberant of the dot.com years by employing a tool many internet start-ups seemed to think belonged to an old-economy paradigm: cash flow.

Denis Gadbois was no kid in a garage when he helped found Mediagrif, the company of which he is now chairman and CEO. He was thirty-five years old, with two bachelor's degrees. The first was in education, from the Université du Québec à Montréal, and he had taught school for five years before going back to school himself, at HEC Montréal, to earn his second degree, in commerce. He then worked in the IT sector, becoming involved in several projects, including one for a homebuilder's association, before acquiring a minority interest in a small Montreal software company.

Gadbois could see the internet boom coming and wanted his company to move into its path. His partners disagreed. They bought out his interest, which added to his start-up capital for a new venture and an idea—for a web-based business-to-business service. The concept was already being developed by one of his new partners, programmer Patrice Breton. The third partner, Pierre Duval, had a solid technology background. When it came time to create the partnership, Gadbois was the only one with injectible capital—love money amounting to $225,000—so he put up all the money, making arrangements with his partners to be compensated by them later.

The combination of skills in the partnership was a strength from the beginning. It had both business acumen and technology smarts. In that mix alone, Mediagrif was ahead of so many technology start-ups (and not just internet-based ones) in which the proprietor's main talent is in creating the novelty that is to be brought to market. A tech start-up is fundamentally, and most commonly, doomed by one of three deep flaws: the idea is a bad one; or a viable idea is brought forward by someone who does not have the business skills to carry that idea forward to commercial fruition; or the idea is innovative and even practical, but not in a way that can support a profitable venture.

Perhaps the single greatest challenge posed by the abundant potential of the internet was how to make money from or through it. There was no problem getting people to sign up for an account with an internet service provider (ISP), to pay for the computer they required to send and receive email and surf the web. Nor was there a problem with getting these same people to use internet software utilities. The problem was getting them to pay for them.

The internet, it must be remembered, was a creature of academia that had been given its initial shove toward global domination by U.S. defence department funding. Only a year before the Mediagrif business plan began to come together, the internet was essentially the land of the free (as in, free utilities and swapped files) and the home of the brave (as in, what's a virus?). In the early years of the World Wide Web, anyone who wished to surf the web need only download a free copy of Netscape's public-domain inspiration, the Mosaic browser, or one of several other available giveaways; even the commercial Netscape browser was then downloaded for free. There were surprisingly few things that the average internet user had to consider paying for beyond the monthly ISP bill.

Internet traffic skyrocketed through the 1990s. Total annual traffic (as measured in data packets) rose from less than 12 million in 1984 (when the Domain Name System came into being) to 21 billion in 1994. And between 1994 and 1998, the number of hosts or routers managing the internet's traffic rose from 1000 to more than 40 million, while the number of internet accounts increased from 30 million to 150 million.

A lot of users. A lot of traffic. A lot of growth. The rise of the internet has often been compared to the nineteenth-century railway boom (often in the context of overbuilt capacity and investment disaster), but it is actually more like a highway system. Because highways, unlike railway tracks, are not proprietary. And once a highway system exists, it presents commercial opportunities that utilize the system, rather than being based on that system. The money is not in operating the highway as a toll road; it's in recognizing the advantages it presents to transportation companies, such as bus lines and trucking fleets, and in capitalizing on spin-off benefits, like the increase in property values around interchanges.

The impact, and the true commercial opportunities, of transformative technologies like the internet are never immediately, transparently evident. A business person seeing the buildout of a highway system might immediately think that the real money was going to be in paving. It would have been difficult to foresee how all that pavement was actually going to generate enormous opportunities for hotel and motel chains catering to private motorists. The internet went through a similar process of moving from the obvious to the inspirational when it came to commercial exploitation. Just like paving companies, the big communications engineering firms that had the technology to build the optical networks and switching systems that were the backbone of the internet rapidly became investment darlings—and just as rapidly vaporized billions in investment capital. Meanwhile, ventures were being launched that were trying to imagine how the internet could be harnessed in a profitable way, how it would or could create opportunities.

Those opportunities were multifold, but at a grossly simple level, from the commercial transaction perspective, there were two opportunities. Property existing in a digital format—images, music, software—could be delivered over the internet, and the purchases managed through it. Most property, however, doesn't exist as data and couldn't be transmogrified into packets and stuffed into optical fibres, then reassembled in three dimensions at the recipient's end of the connection. Nevertheless, the transactional process could be greatly aided and abetted by using the internet as a link between buyer and seller. And the potential to move that process to the internet existed in both the business-to-consumer (B2C) and the business-to-business (B2B) environments.

The trick—and it proved to be one of Houdiniesque proportions—was demonstrating a way to make money out of this transactional shift. It quickly turned out that you could sell many things over the internet, but not necessarily profitably. As Amazon.com rapidly proved, it was not difficult to convince consumers to purchase books, videos, computer games, and other goods from a virtual store. Doing it profitably was another matter, and it took Amazon.com until the fourth quarter of 2001 (albeit as it promised Wall Street) to move into the black for the first time. And some things (such as dog food) proved to be much more difficult to persuade people to buy online rather than off a store shelf. Other brokerage-based businesses, such as travel agencies and securities traders, made the transition to the web, with varying degrees of financial success.

The partners in Mediagrif could see a role for themselves in the commercial possibilities of the internet. They weren't going to sell things themselves over it. Nor were they going to sell or design a program that allowed others to do business on the web. Rather, they were going to create what amounted to private networks that functioned within the public internet realm, which would facilitate transactions in the business-to-business realm.

Success or failure depended not only on creating a product that worked but also on persuading businesses to become clients. Mediagrif demonstrated a prescient understanding that in the world of the web, it was seldom a problem getting people to use something for nothing. The problem was to get them to pay anything for something. It wasn't a matter of people cheating; it was a matter of demonstrating a value that people or businesses were willing to pay for to use. Netscape, for example, had demonstrated how to build massive market share by giving away its browser through free downloads, but by 1997, as competition heated up with Microsoft and its Explorer browser, Netscape began shifting its profitability model away from the browser and in part toward its enterprise software division, which produced products that helped companies manage information flow through their own networks.

Mediagrif understood that the value proposition was easier to make in business-to-business than in business-to-consumer. In many cases, consumer-oriented internet start-ups were offering services that weren't entirely new but, rather, an alternative to an existing bricks-and-mortar experience. Airline tickets could be bought online, or by visiting the local agent's office. Books and CDs and video games similarly could be ordered online, or accessed at the nearest shopping mall. And where there was genuine novelty in the business-to-consumer market, the consumer had to be convinced that whatever was on offer was worth paying for, particularly when spending was discretionary and the goods or service could be had elsewhere.

"Business-to-business is different in that a business has resources to pay for value, unlike a consumer," says Gadbois. "If you're generating business for a company, you're demonstrating value to it, and it will pay for that." While it's true that consumers will pay for demonstrated value, it's generally a different proposition. If the service being offered in a business-to-business environment involves an ongoing aspect of a business, the savings, whether in dollars outlaid or efficiency gains, can be measured and understood. A consumer, on the other hand, isn't buying a television set or a trip to Jamaica online every week. He or she may find the experience convenient, even cheaper, but might not spend money that way again for years—and even if the opportunity arises to shop that way again, the consumer may take a pass, perhaps because he or she happens to be in an actual store when the urge to spend on discretionary items strikes and isn't about to go home to make the purchase online instead. B2B had a much more straightforward value proposition. If a company could see demonstrable benefit, it would pay for what was being offered, and build that benefit into its regular course of business. Mediagrif's first B2B network offering would be The Broker Forum, which deals in electronics components.

As a start-up, Mediagrif knew it didn't have enough money in the bank to maintain itself to the point of positive cash flow. The business plan called for the company to make the value proposition to customers by making its first product available initially for free. A B2B environment requires participants and traffic for it to make sense on a fee basis. Mediagrif wanted companies to experience the product at no expense or risk, be convinced of its value, and then be prepared to pay for the services. At the same time, Mediagrif needed hard data from the product's usage to take to the venture capital market, so that funding for the next stage could be secured.

"We managed our money very diligently," says Gadbois. "We were going to achieve as much as possible with that initial cash so that we could have as much leverage as possible when we went out for venture cap. As a start-up, you generally don't have a lot of leverage. We had objectives in mind for products: the number of clients, key operating metrics, revenues per client.... We wanted to show progress within the initial six months. We needed to grab data showing that people were using them." That data would convince the users that the service was worth paying for, and the venture capitalists that the concept could actually work and was worth financing.

In July 1996, Mediagrif began making the rounds of venture capitalists, choosing the private funding route at this early stage rather than an IPO. The dot.com boom would become famous for IPOs by technology companies without demonstrable revenues, or much hope of generating them, but at the time, the pressure to "do" a public offering was much less prevalent, especially when start-ups had so little to demonstrate in the way of a proven business. It would take Amazon.com almost two years from the date its website opened for business to proceed with an IPO, in May 1997. Mediagrif could imagine an IPO down the road, but for now, private capital was the most practical means to fund the growth toward profitability.

The partners looked only to Quebec for venture cap funds, for the simple reason that they couldn't afford to look anywhere else. They had stretched their seed money to molecular thinness and couldn't swing the expense of the road shows they might otherwise have been tempted to launch.

"Money for an internet company was not as widely available then," says Gadbois. "The other constraint was that, being based in Montreal, we didn't have the resources to be visible in San Francisco's Bay Area, for example. It was difficult for us to meet with U.S.–based VCs [venture capitalists]. We were not generating revenues, the business model was new, and we didn't have money. For the three of us to buy $2000 plane tickets to go to San Francisco and spend two or three days there ... We would have been innovators, if we had, but we didn't have the resources. So we focused on the Quebec VC market, which was very limited, but we were confident that the key operational indicators were positive. The business model looked like it was working and we would be able to convert free users into paying users."

The business model indeed turned out to be convincing, even in the province's relatively shallow pool of venture capital. The partners were presented with three funding options. The typical venture offering at the time was essentially a debenture, in which rates as high as 14 percent would have to be paid. Mediagrif didn't want to be a borrower: It wanted the venture cap's support to be converted into equity interest. Mediagrif ended up choosing an offer in which a total of $500,000 was made available to them, and would be convertible to common shares at a ratio dependent on Mediagrif's ability to meet performance targets. If Mediagrif did well, in two years the investment would convert into 13 percent of the company's equity. In the worst case, the partners would surrender one-quarter of Mediagrif.

The first portion, of $200,000, would become available in December 1996; the remaining $300,000 would follow, in March 1997. It was Mediagrif's plan to begin charging for The Broker Forum service on April 1, 1997. The search for venture cap was a near-run thing for the partners and their six employees. "Before we got the first cheque," says Gadbois, "we were one week away from not being able to meet the payroll."

But once they had the money, the partners managed it so well that they hadn't used it all by the time the second injection was ready to be made. By then, they had the data they were looking for on traffic on The Broker Forum, and were confident that they could convert the free users into paying customers beginning April 1. The resulting cash flow, and the funds remaining from the first venture cap injection, could keep them moving forward. "We took a gamble and refused the second investment, of $300,000," says Gadbois. "We were initiating the process of charging, and it was do-or-die. If people converted, we would be able to finance ourselves. If our assumptions were not working, we were in deep trouble. We took that gamble and it paid out. But it put a lot of stress on the relationship with the VC."

Declining investment already proffered was not the standard internet start-up practice. It ruffled feathers on the VC side for two reasons. First, by declining to accept the full investment, Mediagrif was limiting the opportunity of the VC to participate in its success. Second, if Mediagrif was wrong about its cash-flow projections, the VC's initial investment would be placed in jeopardy should Mediagrif then founder. But Mediagrif was sure of its business plan, and of its numbers. It really didn't need the additional $300,000.

The Broker Forum turned out to be the success that the partners predicted. As of 2004, the Forum was boasting 43 million lines of available stock, with 3025 members generating more than 3.2 million product searches and 1.5 million bid requests per month on the network. Eighty percent of the members had built The Broker Forum into their daily business operations. The partners had been right: If they could demonstrate value in the business environment, companies would pay.

From there, Mediagrif watched "internet mania" (as Gadbois puts it) blossom. Mediagrif was very young, but in a very young industry, it was now an established player. It had a product that worked and generated cash, a willing source of venture capital that was still holding $300,000 the partners had declined to use, and a business plan that was fully executable. The company's approach called for new specialty B2B networks to be created by Mediagrif itself, or acquired. In early 1998, Mediagrif was prepared to make its first acquisition, a network dedicated to computer equipment.

At that point, Mediagrif's venture capitalists returned to the table. "The VCs said, 'We're going to give you the $300,000 you didn't use last time, then $700,000 on top of that.' At the end of the process, they put in a million dollars and got 22 percent of the company. We ended up with more than a million in the bank account, and were generating cash. We were in a fairly good position. The market value of the company through this second investment phase was confirmed at Can$10 million."

As Mediagrif closed its second investment phase, the internet's popularity continued to mushroom. "Everyone wanted to be a player, to have a share," says Gadbois. At the beginning of 1999, Mediagrif's capitalization was confirmed at $40 million, attracting further investment. "We started to develop partnerships in the industry with larger players, collecting money from different partners, up to $30 and $35 million, who wanted to start up joint ventures with us. We had more than $20 million in the bank, were involved in multiple industries, and had a slight profit. We had to decide on the next step. That led us to the IPO."

"Mediagrif is a textbook case of a dot.com company that's a real company," says Tony Dimnik, an accounting professor at the Queen's School of Business. For a new venture to meet the definition of "real," Dimnik lays out three basic criteria:

1. Is it an actual business? In other words, does it have cash flow potential? Many dot.com start-ups, as noted, were industriously producing goods or services that no one would pay for.
2. Is there a competitive advantage? Can the company do something that no one else can? If anyone can do it, someone will, and there goes your cash flow potential.
3. Who are the people running the company? Competitive advantage erodes over time and so a company needs the people and culture that will continuously reinvent the business. The founders of a company and the people they hire have to keep coming up with new ways of creating competitive advantages, which in turn drive cash flow.

Dimnik sees parallels between Mediagrif and an online legal service on whose board he served. The approach to cash flow management in the legal service was similar to that of Mediagrif, and so was its inherent business conservatism, so rare in the dot.com frenzy. In the case of the legal service, says Dimnik, "it was so prudent that it actually missed the dot.com IPO window," and was ultimately acquired by an American competitor.

With the decision in early 2000 to proceed with an IPO, Mediagrif had at last come to the typical dot.com start-up point of payback. The IPO was when the ground-floor investors—the founders, the senior executives, the VCs—cashed in their tickets with a public offering. Pricing the IPO was something of a dark art, but the success of an IPO was often judged on the basis of getting the offering price wrong. That's because fortunes were waiting to be made on the "pop," the immediate leap in share price in aftermarket trading, which allowed insiders to sell their shares or exercise lucrative options. Investors had been popping dot.com IPOs at a frantic rate, and doing so with companies that had little to demonstrate in the way of revenues or clear earnings potential. Compared with many of them, Mediagrif was almost old economy. Mediagrif's business model involved financing operations and meeting capital requirements through cash flow and from issuing stock. And it maintained a positive cash balance to finance new opportunities and fund operations.

Unfortunately, Mediagrif's IPO plan had the worst possible timing—not from the perspective of its business plan, but from the state of the IPO market. The company was set to go public on the NASDAQ in May 2000. That spring, the NASDAQ went through its now-infamous meltdown, reaching an all-time high of 5048.62 on March 10, only to shed one-third of its value by April 14. The day before Mediagrif's partners were scheduled to meet with the firm handling the IPO and set the price, Intel Corp. posted discouraging news, and once this bellwether tech stock had been factored into the general negativity of the markets, Mediagrif decided to hold off on the price selection. Two weeks later, Mediagrif's IPO was shelved, though not abandoned altogether. The company had strong fundamentals, and in early October, a window of opportunity opened long enough for the IPO to go ahead on the TSX and gain the company $53.1 million. The timing turned out to be brilliant. A few weeks later, Nortel missed the consensus earnings estimate of analysts by a penny on its third-quarter results, and the panic selling on the TSX was such that it shut down the entire market. Mediagrif had slipped through before investor sentiment on internet-related technology stocks might have made an IPO impossible for many, many months, if not years. "We were the last internet company IPO until late 2003," Gadbois says. "The window was so narrow we had to go through it sideways. We had showed that our business model was working, that we were good at executing."

Today, Mediagrif has B2B networks in nine areas: electronics components, wines and spirits, computer equipment, telecommunications equipment, automotive aftermarket parts, truck parts, government e-tendering (which includes the MERX electronic tendering system used by the government of Canada), medical equipment, and IT parts and equipment. It also provides e-commerce services to companies, with 160 of its 350 employees being software developers and Java-language specialists. Revenues are approaching $50 million. At year-end 2005 (March 31), Mediagrif had almost $100 million in assets, including more than $50 million in cash and cash equivalents.

The irrational exuberance of the dot.com investment boom had been wickedly skewered post facto in 2000 by E*Trade, which ran television commercials showing a sorrowful chimp named Mister Brooks riding a pony through a tumbleweed-strewn internet ghost town. Mister Brooks never laid eyes on a broken-down Mediagrif sign, because the company hadn't even hung one out yet in the public markets. The boom-bust came and went before the Montreal company emerged on the TSX, functioning and profitable.

Since going public in October 2000, "nothing else happened," Gadbois says—at least, not from the perspective of start-up funding. "We are generating free cash. The company is not leveraged at all. There is $52 million still in the bank. With availability of borrowing, we could go to $100 million."

In April 2005, Claude Thibault joined Mediagrif as its new CFO. He came over from a Shell Chemicals joint venture in Montreal; before that he had been involved with a number of companies in the internet-multimedia-software realm, having been an investment banker with Merrill Lynch Canada. He arrived at the company practically flush with opportunity, not to mention cash flow.

Thibault confirms one of the great strengths of the Mediagrif business model: "We are a fixed cost business." Operating its B2B networks has relatively finite expenses. As you add customers, the revenues increase, but the costs of running the network don't grow correspondingly. Little wonder that Mediagrif has been so successful in generating cash. Both the fixed-cost nature of the business and Mediagrif's handsome cash flow make for a potent combination in the pursuit of growth. Any new customer it adds to its networks through organic growth fuels the cash flow. And customers added onto the existing Mediagrif network through the acquisition of competing companies boost cash flow with little additional operating expense. Acquisitions truly create more efficient networks in Mediagrif's case, and they have become a principal means of growth for the company.

Having the money in the bank certainly makes acquisitions possible. But finding good acquisitions has been difficult at times for Mediagrif. For one thing, there are not a lot of early-stage-growth companies around that fit a traditional acquisition bill. "Start-ups at this stage of the game are not as promising as they were in the past," says Thibault of Mediagrif's B2B networking field, "when it was a more open marketplace. The chance of a newcomer becoming a significant competitor is becoming lower and lower."

Nevertheless, Mediagrif has plenty of potential acquisitions to choose from among established players. The B2B markets in which it participates are crowded with competitors. "There are thousands of players out there, in very fragmented markets," says Thibault. "We're often the leader, but we don't necessarily have a majority of the business. We might have 50 percent, or 15 percent." All that fragmentation provides innumerable acquisition opportunities that will add more customers to Mediagrif's existing networks. But Mediagrif must sort through those opportunities and find ones that don't harm Mediagrif's financial strengths. In growing in part through acquisitions after the NASDAQ implosion, Mediagrif had to contend with takeover targets that were suffering from the delusion that their earnings multiples were, say, double that of Mediagrif.

Acquisition targets, says Thibault, "are not all as profitable as we are—in fact, they rarely are—which is a stumbling block. When you buy a company that is not as good as you are, you have to have a strategy to turn it around. You don't want it to be dilutive.

We are a very disciplined buyer," he emphasizes. "We have turned down acquisitions because the asking price was too high. If you pay too much for the profits you're getting, it's not a good buy." Dimnik concurs: "You can always buy top-line growth, but it's much tougher finding investments that generate a return higher than the cost of capital."

Mediagrif pays close attention both to return on investment and return on sales as it gauges the benefits of a particular acquisition target. "Right now, we're at about 20 percent of free cash flow from sales," says Thibault. "If we buy companies without the same return on sales ... We'd rather not go there. Last year we did three acquisitions and they were all successes for those reasons."

All the same, finding good acquisitions is such a challenge that the company has to a degree concluded that the best investment it can make is in itself, as it buys back shares. "Year in, year out," says Thibault, "at the current pace, we're making $10 million a year. Even if we were to buy back 5 percent of shares in a year, we'd still be cash flow positive." Mediagrif is reaching the point, says Thibault, that "it may be that target companies want our shares instead of cash, to ride on our own potential. Our stock is a valuable acquisition currency."

Denis Gadbois looks back on the rapid success of Mediagrif, sets aside the irrational exuberance of the dot.com boom-bust, and draws basic lessons for launching a new venture. "When you are in a starting mode," he advises, "you need to get your credibility as high as possible, or you don't have any leverage, once the two to three years you were being paid to develop a bright idea is over. People will need to be convinced that your idea will generate money. You need additional data to increase their level of confidence."

It's a lesson that extends far beyond the internet. Mediagrif didn't just make a successful go of it, without depending on overheated, uncritical investors to provide the capital. It made a go of it by doing precisely what it set out to do.

"When we moved offices within the same building about a year and a half ago," says Gadbois, "I put my hands on the original business plan that was given to venture capitalists. It still applied. Ninety-five percent of our execution is in line with what we set up in 1996."

Gadbois, of course, is still with the company, as is original partner Pierre Duval. But the youngest of the three, Patrice Breton, the programmer who developed the first network, has cashed in and moved on. "He's driving around town in a sports car," is how Gadbois puts it, with a distinctively dot.com measure of pride. At least something about Mediagrif fits the standard template of success in the internet revolution.

The Deloitte perspective

Attracting capital and managing finances

The partners of Mediagrif faced two fundamental questions regarding finances: first, how to raise money to finance growth, given the various stages of the life cycle of a company; and second (and more important), *where* to spend that money.

Companies planning to raise capital must execute their financial plan skilfully and conservatively. There is nothing spectacular about what Mediagrif did, but there are also no mistakes. They stuck to their business model from the beginning, and were very disciplined about using their cash. They hired only the people they could support with the money they had available. Many other companies went on a spending spree, thinking once they used all the money, there would be more coming.

Mediagrif's founders went from starting up with their own money to using venture capital, and they did not take all the money available to them. Since going public, they have not strayed from their business model. They did not bend to the pressures of analysts and markets to make acquisitions merely for the sake of acquisitions.

As the Mediagrif story illustrates, attracting capital today is a lot harder than it was a decade ago for emerging companies looking to fund a business plan. Such companies are well advised to follow Mediagrif's example and focus on these key elements:

Plan the company's finance strategy:

- Determine precisely the financial, operational, and market-related wants and needs of the company by examining all areas of the business.
- Build a strategic plan that details what the company intends to accomplish and how it plans to achieve this.
- Identify the most appropriate sources of capital and investment options to pursue.

Prepare for the funding process:

- Highlight the quality and support of the management and organizational structure of the company as evidence that investments will be successful.
- Show investors that the company has an attractive and sustainable business model.
- Validate the financial package with supporting financial documents.

Engage identified investors:

- Obtain the best deal by talking with several potential investors, thereby creating a competitive setting for the transaction.
- Negotiate the deal and collect information of the negotiation experience to enable reflection and learning.

Once capital has been injected into the company, be it through debt or equity, the next step is to manage those funds. Successfully managing finances involves maintaining a healthy and sustainable mix of three categories: investments, cash flow, and returns to shareholders:

- *When to invest?* Consider investing in projects where the company's valuable formula can be sustained with acceptable risk levels throughout the project's life cycle.
- *How much cash should the company maintain?* A company has to maintain an optimal balance of liquidity by assessing the trade-off between the benefits and the cost of liquidity. An adequate amount of assets in cash is needed to ensure efficient running of day-to-day business.
- *How much in returns should be provided to stockholders, and when?* A company must decide how much is appropriate to pay its stockholders to maintain their confidence and continued investment in the company.

8 Laying solid foundations

Designing the right organization and processes to support growth

PCL Construction Group of Companies

Canada's 50 Best Managed Companies winner, 1994–1999, 2001, 2002
Named to Platinum Club, 2003

Out on Ottawa's LeBreton Flats, west of the Parliament Buildings, one of the most important, and most exciting, new public structures in Canada was opened to the public in May 2005. Designed by Moriyama & Teshima Architects, the new Canadian War Museum is a multidimensional structure of almost 450,000 square feet, displaying everything from large military vehicles to war art. Even with an exhibition area that greatly expands on the museum's old cramped quarters in the former Public Archives building on Sussex Drive, about 90 percent of the new building is devoted to uses other than exhibition, serving a modern museum's many needs: proper climate-controlled storage, classrooms, a theatre, a much-improved library and research facilities, and an internet outreach program, to name a few features.

It is a source of considerable pride for its general contractor, PCL Construction Group of Companies of Edmonton. "A project like the war museum is rare," says PCL vice-president Dwight Brown, the company's district manager in Ottawa. "It's a national monument. It's very important to the company because it's noticed across the country. You're extremely concerned about the schedule, and the quality. And it's a rare job where it touches everyone involved on a personal level. The interesting thing with a project like this is that you attract the better trades, because they want to be involved in it. Everybody has taken pride in it. And it was a very complicated job, with the sloped walls, and the grass roof."

Some three hundred thousand visitors are expected to pass through the museum's doors every year. Their focus rightfully is on the content of this landmark achievement in museum design. They aren't really thinking about who built it. They are most certainly unaware that many signature buildings in the greater Ottawa area—among them the Corel Centre, City Hall, World Exchange Plaza, the Ottawa campus of La Cité collégiale, and (across the river) the National Archives Gatineau Preservation Centre—were, like the new museum, built by PCL Construction Group of Companies, whose parent holding company is based in Edmonton. PCL is Canada's largest general contractor and one of the largest in North America. And if they flew into Ottawa on their visit from any number of major centres—Vancouver, Calgary, Saskatoon, Toronto, Halifax, even Denver, to name just a few—they passed through an airport with terminals and other significant facilities built by PCL.

And these significant public structures are only the beginning of PCL's increasing—and increasingly diversified—presence in construction. There's not much that PCL won't propose to build (and not just build, but service and maintain). PCL built Saskatchewan Indian Federated College in Regina; a twenty-seven-thousand-seat soccer stadium for California State University; the Canadian side of the Blue Water Bridge, linking Port Huron, Michigan, and Point Edward, Ontario; the Air Canada Centre in Toronto, and the National Trade Centre, and the Eaton's renovation at Toronto Eaton Centre, and BCE Place and Galleria, and Scotia Plaza, and Canada Life headquarters, and on and on. A remarkable amount of public space and identifiable skyline has risen from the ground—and sometimes plunged underground—through the efforts and expertise of PCL.

But as Brown counsels, the showcase buildings are only the tip of PCL's construction iceberg. "We have a recognition within the construction industry because of high-profile projects. But most of our projects are under a million dollars. People don't recognize us on that end of it. In Ottawa, we may have twelve major projects over $10 million during any one year, but another sixty to seventy under that, with most of those less than $5 million. We don't get recognized for that. As far as a household name, unless you're in the industry, you don't know us."

He laughs at the fact that he'll meet people who've seen a PCL sign on a construction site somewhere in Canada, then see it again on a project in Florida. They'll come back home and say, surprised, "Hey, that was you guys!"

There's no question that the PCL sign continues to pop up in new places. The interesting question is, why?

Why do enterprises seek growth? That companies should grow is such a natural assumption that the reason for growth often is never articulated. But why, exactly, is bigger also better?

It's a good question, because so many entrepreneurs meet their Waterloo in a reflexive drive for revenue growth. Indeed, many large companies have seemed to grow through acquisitions and mergers not because of any underlying business imperative but, rather, as an expression of a corporate hubris best summed up as "because we can." Diversification can become an end unto itself; corporations can turn into holding companies of disconnected enterprises, ostensibly to hedge against downturns in any single business sector. But even where synergies were said to be the objective, benefits often failed to materialize. Business history is littered with examples of what now seems like testosterone-driven expansions of corporate kingdoms—which, like the Roman Empire, proved to be too widespread, too vulnerable around the perimeter to attacks by agile, ruthless competitors, to rule and prosper.

Driving the top line by whatever means certainly can produce many benefits, above and beyond the increased revenues (and, hopefully, profits). Growth can be the result of forays into new markets, and new products and services. It can produce increased market share that delivers industry leadership. And with a new venture, growth is a necessity as revenues are ramped up and returns are secured on the initial investment.

But why exactly does an established enterprise press for growth—particularly if it means diversifying into areas of business in which the company does not have an historic role or core competencies? For some companies, the decision to seek significant growth (as opposed to incremental increases in revenues) derives from a recognition that their main area of business is experiencing a slowdown or actual decline, or is beset by unacceptably low margins, and that prosperity lies in other, more innovative, directions. Sometimes companies reinvent themselves in search of growth after creating a fresh business plan—for example, the way IBM transformed itself from being fundamentally a manufacturer of computers to a service-oriented company.

Many companies have grown through a variety of strategies, but always with the goal of expanding on their core competencies. No matter how large they become, they're still recognizable as a growing version of the original enterprise. Edmonton's PCL Construction Group of Companies is a case in point. Founded in 1906 by Ernest Poole, the company was being run by his sons George and John when it was acquired in 1977 and turned into an employee-owned enterprise. Revenues were about $300 million in 1977. Today, PCL is the largest general contracting organization in Canada, and one of the largest in the United States. It has experienced tremendous growth in recent years. In 1997, the holding company was realizing revenues of $1.7 billion. By 2002, that had increased to $3 billion, and it expected to exceed $3.8 billion in 2005 and reach $5 billion in 2006. Its employee ranks surged from 4000 in 2002 to almost 5900 in 2004.

In 2004, PCL Construction came out ahead in the rankings of Canada's top contractors, as compiled by *Heavy Construction News,* based on sales volume. It's a winning streak some twenty-five years strong. With a dollar-volume lead of about 3:1 over its nearest competitor, and its own sales soaring, PCL is unlikely to give up that title any time soon. But this would amount to little more than gigantism were it not for the company's reputation for excellence. It ranked so consistently and persistently in the Best Managed rankings that it is now a member of the Platinum Club, and it has also ranked among the 50 Best Companies to Work for in Canada, as compiled by the *Globe and Mail*'s *Report on Business* magazine.

In PCL's case, the most obvious answer to the question "Why grow?" is opportunity. There's business out there, things large and small to be built, new opportunities in growing industry sectors which PCL has been able to identify and exploit. But the main reason president and CEO Ross Grieve cites for pursuing growth is not what intuitively occurs to most business people.

Essentially, a company must grow so that its valued employees have their own opportunities to grow. The processes PCL employs to drive growth, the way the organization has been structured, revolve around providing opportunity for internal talent.

It's almost a chicken-and-egg puzzle: do you grow to make people happy, or do you make people happy so that you can grow? Study PCL, and try to decide. As a private company owned by its employees, each participating shareholder—and more than 80 percent of its two thousand salaried employees have a piece of PCL—has an individual stake in the collective success. PCL's strategies for growth are diverse, but the means to achieve growth come back to a simple formula.

"If employees perform extraordinarily well," PCL stated in celebrating its twenty-fifth anniversary of employee ownership in 2002, "company performance is more likely to be extraordinary, and that translates into high share value for employees." PCL believes research that indicates employee ownership promotes faster growth and greater stability than private or public ownership is correct, and that PCL is living proof.

"We are convinced that employee ownership made the difference during tough times," said Grieve in marking the 2002 anniversary, "and has helped us to really excel during good times." Despite two serious recessions since 1977 which battered the construction industry, PCL has always been profitable, and has always paid a dividend to its employee-owners.

"All organizations, particularly ones like ours, must grow," says Grieve. "In that way, more people are coming into your organization than are leaving." For Grieve, growth is a natural response to the prerogative of providing opportunity within an organization, because opportunity is the key to ensuring strength in the human capital of an enterprise. "Young people are looking for career development, and challenges, and upward mobility. They will stall out if you don't give them opportunities, and could end up going to work for competitors."

The employee ranks of great companies are always prime targets for headhunters. Not everyone can be accommodated (or deserves to be) in the upward march of seniority, as the management pyramid steadily narrows. But the loss of good people is disruptive. Replacements must be recruited and trained, client relationships are damaged, and if the departing employee lands with a competitor, you've effectively given the enemy its weapons training. The human capital in which a company has so carefully invested ends up being an asset for an adversary offering opportunities that it cannot.

In the construction industry, a business that specializes in multimillion-dollar projects must go where the work is, whether it's to build an airport, an arena, a hotel, or an entertainment complex. Winning bids take it into new geographic territories, and as a project unfolds, a company has two choices: to complete the job and then withdraw to bid on similar work elsewhere, or to use the job as a beachhead in a new market, and establish a permanent presence there. In PCL's case, the latter strategy has been adopted in several circumstances, becoming one important mechanism by which growth is achieved, systematically, and with minimal risk exposure.

"Our economy has been good for the last number of years, in Canada and the United States," says Grieve. "The external forces of economy have allowed us to grow, and we've been able to get more than our fair share of business. We've made decisions to expand into new geographies. We might enter a new geography by securing a new project in an area where we don't have a full-service office. While we're there for a couple years on the project, we test-market the place. And if there are opportunities in that district, we'll move in that direction.

"San Diego opened up for us a few years ago in doing a project. We've now converted it to a full-service branch. We've been in the Hawaiian islands for about seven years, and have had a very successful run there. We built the convention centre there first, then exited, but we were invited back. It convinced us we could compete in Hawaii, and we've set up an operations office in Honolulu.

"We were working in and out of Atlantic Canada since the late 1960s, but never had a permanent presence. We serviced it at first out of Winnipeg, and more recently from Toronto and Ottawa." In February 1999, for example, PCL scored its first ever P-3 (public-private partnership) contract to build fifteen schools in Nova Scotia. "We then had a big opportunity with the cleanup of Halifax Harbour," says Grieve. PCL set up a new district office in Dartmouth in August 2002 in anticipation of the awarding of the $175 million Halifax Harbour Solutions Project, a P-3 consortium in which PCL was the contractor for a new waste treatment facility that would put an end to the city pumping about 180 million litres of raw sewage into the harbour each day. The contract was signed in October and was scheduled to start in December, but the project was delayed, as the city and the consortium could not agree on who would be legally liable if treated sewage did not meet federal standards. In June 2003, the deal fell apart. "That didn't go ahead for us," says Grieve, "but we had put people on the ground there, and picked up work as a result." PCL's work in Halifax has included the new airport terminal, and a twelve-storey residential tower for navy personnel as well as a new training facility for the government's recent order for the new Sikorsky helicopters.

PCL's breadth of construction work verges on bewildering. In the spring of 2005, you could find seventeen projects on the go without progressing farther than the letter B in the alphabetical listing. The first consonant in the alphabet served up, among others, the Bubba Gump Shrimp Company theme restaurant at the Mall of America in Bloomington, Minnesota; the BMO computer centre in Barrie, Ontario; a bridge at Blackmud Creek in Edmonton, Alberta; the Buckley Air Force Base chapel centre in Aurora, Colorado; and the seven-hundred-thousand-square-foot development at Bay and Dundas Streets for the Ryerson School of Business in Toronto.

Elsewhere in the alphabet and on the planet, PCL was building a three-level subterranean parking garage with a baseball field atop it for Caltech in Pasadena, California; erecting Canadian Tire and Best Buy stores in Vancouver; expanding the Central Arizona Project water treatment plant in Mesa, Arizona; providing Cape Girardeau, Missouri, with a design-build courthouse; constructing a 20,500-square-foot clubhouse for Crandon Park Golf Course in Key Biscayne, Florida; adding 400,000 square feet (including the Carlo Fidani Peel Regional Cancer Centre) to Credit Valley Hospital in Mississauga, Ontario; building Crown City Center, a six-storey class-A office tower with retail and dining space and an adjoining six-level parking garage in Pasadena, California … and we haven't even left the letter C yet.

Expertise in construction areas such as airports, hospitals, and schools leads to similar work in new locales, causing the company to increase business in a specialty area while also moving into new territories. With airports alone, PCL has developed into an industry leader since tackling the new Calgary International Airport in the 1970s. Denver International Airport, completed in 1994, was a showcase effort which brought PCL further work from that airport and has since seen it tackle, among other projects, Vancouver International Airport's terminal and, in a joint venture with the design-build firm Aecon Inc., the new main terminal of Pearson International in Toronto (among other Pearson components). PCL also built a new traffic control tower for Seattle-Tacoma International Airport, added eighty thousand square feet (in a joint venture with Maxam Contracting Ltd.) to Diefenbaker International Airport in Saskatoon, and secured (with Maxam) three of four major contracts for the redevelopment of Edmonton International Airport's terminal.

The list goes on. Moreover, we haven't even begun to describe the full scope of PCL's business. The above projects are the ones the general public can see and identify. PCL is also busy in the heavy industrial sector, not only building things but securing contracts for servicing and maintenance. Expansion, Grieve explains, has come in "identifying growing industries that we want to penetrate more significantly. The heavy industrial sector in Alberta is one." While PCL "has been in it for decades," the company saw growing opportunities in the oil, gas, petrochemical, forestry, and mining sectors if it could adapt to meet them, by investing in plant and equipment to capitalize on growth, particularly around the oil sands boom. Pipe fabrication was one area in which it was vital to have capabilities. In anticipation of securing new business in Alberta from companies such as Syncrude, Suncor Energy, Dow Chemical, and Nova Chemicals, PCL invested significantly in its existing pipe fabrication facility at Nisku, Alberta, upgrading through additional space, improved material handling, and new welding technology. "We now have in our opinion one of the best pipe fabrication facilities in North America," says Grieve.

PCL recognized the opportunities in industrial modules for these Alberta resource companies. PCL had been in the module business since the late 1970s, and recently invested in a twenty-five-acre facility at Nisku where up to one hundred modules can be constructed simultaneously. "We bought and developed land where we can assemble massive modules in the south that can be hauled on heavy-load vehicles to plant sites such as Syncrude, Suncor, and Albion Sands," Grieve explains.

PCL also turned to acquisitions for growth in capabilities. "In the last ten years, we've made ten acquisitions," says Grieve. "By our character, we're not acquisitors. But these were all strategic, in order to position ourselves for what we saw coming."

Among the things PCL saw coming was a lengthy boom from the oil sands. "There is incredible capital spending in Alberta, billions in projects for oil sands for the next fifteen years. We bought two companies in Alberta to expand our sectoral coverage in heavy industry. One was Intracon, an electrical contractor, and we didn't have any in-house capability." PCL also recognized that once plants were built, they would need to be serviced and maintained. This takes the form of both maintenance shutdowns and ongoing preventive maintenance as the plants run 24-7. "We've been doing service and maintenance for years, but in a smaller way." To ramp up quickly, PCL purchased Melloy and Associates, a shutdown and maintenance contractor.

PCL also wanted to diversify its heavy industrial operations. Even with the projected oil sands boom, markets are cyclical, and to limit its reliance on Alberta, PCL pursued similar work in the United States through acquisitions. In May 2002, it bought the construction division of Fisher-Klosterman, Inc., in the Bakersfield, California, oil field area. Now operating as PCL Industrial Services, Inc., the Bakersfield acquisition brought aboard considerable experience in the construction of oil and gas pipelines, water plants, oil dehydration facilities, and steam plants used in processing heavy crude oil. In late 2003, PCL also acquired Teton Industrial Group (which began operating under PCL as Teton Industrial Construction), an Atlanta-based firm that works on power plants and petrochemical and oil gas infrastructure through a large part of America.

PCL has been experiencing a period of heady growth, both in revenues and company size. It's gone well partly because PCL wasn't trying to solve problems through gigantism. You cannot grow your way out of trouble, but you can certainly grow your way into it. "Growth is a necessity, but it should be done in a controlled way," says Grieve. "You have no business growing if you're having troubles in your existing situations."

As Grieve has noted, a prime driver of growth has been the desire to attract and retain high-quality employees by offering fresh opportunities and room for personal advancement. If a company is going to grow in an orderly and profitable way, and harness growth as an incentive to employees to remain with the company and help everyone excel together, it is going to need a compatible organization, and processes that can support the mutual goal. For Grieve, the employee-ownership model has been critical to PCL's achievements.

At last count, as noted, over 80 percent of PCL's permanent salaried employees were company shareholders. That works out to about 1750 people with a personal stake in PCL's success or failure. Participants first must pass through a six-month probationary period, at which point a supervisor can recommend that they be offered shares. As seniority increases, so do the opportunities to invest. And the employee must actually buy the shares—they're not handed out as bonuses. There is no aftermarket for these shares. They cannot be sold to third parties or to other members of the company. Should you leave the company, the shares must be sold back to PCL. They're also automatically redeemed when an employee turns sixty-four. An annual dividend can be paid at the discretion of the company, and today, one has been granted in every year since employee ownership was instituted in 1977.

"That has really contributed to our growth," Grieve says of the employee ownership. "It has given us a very stable and very committed executive, senior management and mid-management. We've experienced very low turnover in those positions."

Tony Dimnik, an accounting professor at Queen's School of Business, has seen numerous examples of the employee-owner model. They tend to share a common challenge: "As the company grows and becomes more successful, there is increasing pressure from within to go public. The more controlled the shares are, the greater the pressure becomes to realize capital gains in share ownership, especially as more people approach retirement age. One of the main reasons Microsoft went public was to give employees a vehicle to capture the capital gains. The company could probably have funded its growth from operating cash flows."

So far, PCL has avoided the IPO route. "We have an internal joke about the employee ownership being the golden handcuffs," says Dwight Brown. "I think it's great. We've been in Ottawa for fifteen years, and we still have most of the people we started with." He notes that it doesn't only make individual shareholders more dedicated to their own success: "When you have an interest in the company, you take an interest in the other employees around you."

In the wisdom and experience of Ross Grieve, if you wish "to have a growing organization, with a management team in which people are moving up in a proper way, you have to pay attention to succession. Senior management has to be focused on succession planning, ensuring that young people are moving up rapidly enough, are learning the business, are gaining management experience, so that they can take the reins when others exit. You need to be hiring the best people you can and investing in their professional development."

To that end, in 1987, the company established "PCL College of Construction," a training department active in twenty-five locations, providing both internal and external training. Seminars are conducted by full-time staff, and the PCL approach includes remote training, and aids such as books and videos. Participants are taught soft skills in general business areas, as well as technical skills specific to the construction industry.

As PCL grew significantly in recent years, it accelerated the development programs for supervisory and management staff. "We believe that the employee-supervisor relationship is the single most important factor in employee retention and development," PCL has stated. "We also believe that successful growth can only come from a strong organization, and competent supervisors/management is the core of that strength."

PCL began rolling out a supervisory training development program, with its first three instruction modules focused on recruiting and hiring, orientation of new employees, and providing ongoing career feedback to employees. In 2002, two more modules were added: face-to-face communication, and mentoring and coaching. PCL reports that these modules proved so popular that they were opened up to salaried, non-supervisory staff as well.

PCL runs both a leadership program and a construction school of excellence every year. "Supervisory training programs are crucial to ensuring all our people are properly supervised and developing well," says Grieve. The training process also allows the company to "identify future stars, to have new leaders coming up all the time." All twenty-nine PCL operating centres have some kind of teaching facility for its "College of Construction," and PCL encourages employees to engage in both internal and external education programs. It has also developed career development guides to show newcomers how they can work their way up in the organization along specific career paths.

"PCL has gone to the trouble of having a corporate mission and a vision, and of developing education systems," says Dimnik. "It has aligned its reward systems with the goals of the company, in what we call 'goal congruence.' If the company does well, you do well."

Dwight Brown is a first-class example of how PCL has developed talent from within. When he joined PCL in 1980, he was a carpenter working in the field. "PCL really looks at its people and challenges them," Dwight says. "Speaking from experience, if it sees something in you, it puts a lot of effort into making you go where you can go. If you take the challenges this company puts in front of you, you can go far. I was able to rise to vice-president."

"Adding value" has been a PCL rallying cry in its recent years of growth. Back in 1992, PCL established an initiative called QUEST to provide focus for a corporate goal of continuous improvement. It has since expanded with a ten-person corporate QUEST action team (known as CQAT), drawn in 2002 from different regions and functions across PCL.

The QUEST initiative addresses both internal and external customers. Internally, PCL wants all employees to be able to identify their internal customers, to help them meet individual and collective needs. "There should be camaraderie, trust, and respect among leadership teams," Grieve elaborates. "People should work well together—sharing, pitching in when somebody needs help. We're an 'all for one, one for all' organization."

With its external customers (and partners), PCL has identified three distinct groups: subcontractors and suppliers, prime and subconsultants, and owners. "Our goal is to have all of our subcontractors and suppliers view PCL as a business partner who treats them fairly and with respect, and who is concerned with their success, as well as with the success of the project," PCL states. "The benefit to PCL is that our subcontractors will give us preferential pricing, making PCL more competitive. In turn, we can pass on a greater value to our clients."

PCL wants prime and subconsultants "to view PCL as a business partner who they respect, and as a contractor who they can trust to deliver their design with attention to quality and 'completeness'; who recognizes design issues early in the process, and who contributes an expedient and amicable solution to the benefit of all parties; who adds value by helping them to enhance their relationships with the client; and who will help them to minimize their expensive operation and administration costs, and to maximize their ability to get the design items that are important to them into the final project at a minimum expense." PCL identifies the benefit to itself as having prime and subconsultants who "see us as the contractor of choice—the one that they recommend to their clients over all others."

Finally, PCL aims to have clients who view the company "as a partner who understands their business and who thinks innovatively to add value to their overall project." The benefit to PCL? Again, clients will see PCL as the contractor of choice, and will also be willing to pay for value-added services PCL offers, rather than settling for a lower-priced commodity.

In 2002, PCL began instituting a new "vision, values and guiding principles statement" across all operations. It set before the company the goal of becoming "the most respected builder, renowned for excellence, leadership and unsurpassed value." It introduced five core values—honesty, integrity, respect, dynamic culture, and passion—"to focus our employees on the values which we believe help us to maintain our status as a construction leader in the competitive construction industry ... both as a builder and as an employer." And it introduced eight new guiding principles (ownership, teamwork, mutual obligation, safety, effective communication, diversity, mobility, and social responsibility). PCL believes that "by living our vision, we will live and reinforce the PCL brand."

The corporate world has produced plenty of vision statements and the like which have turned out to be little more than lofty words. PCL has been conscious of not allowing its value-management process to become a self-contained exercise in verbiage. When the corporate QUEST action team reported its findings in August 2002, it noted that, with PCL's industry in general, "many of our markets are over supplied with capable construction contractors (especially in the U.S.), and increasingly, we must rely on our reputation, experience, relationships, name recognition, etc. (i.e., factors other than price), to get us to the table in short-list competitions and to win work."

All involved in the action team review "agreed that differentiating ourselves from our competition is more than a buzz word. It is the key to our continued success and future growth." And "living our vision," they concluded, was key to the success of having a PCL brand.

Branding has been important as a rallying point for PCL as a corporate entity. But that cohesion also requires rigorous attention to corporate structure. When a company is growing at the rate of

PCL, spreading geographically at the same time, operating as distinct business units under a holding company umbrella, and growing in some cases by acquiring other companies, it's more than possible for the enterprise to become an amorphous collection of independent operations with their own way of doing things, without consistency or proper accountability across the organization.

"We've had record years, and we're running very well," says Grieve. "I believe our success is directly related to the effort we've put into making sure we have the right corporate structure." Corporate governance has been evaluated and designed from the board all the way down to the operational level. "As CEO," says Grieve, "I have group presidents who look after regions and individual operating companies. From the holding company level, they oversee the independent operating companies. They ensure that those companies are in themselves properly structured and governed—dealing with risk elements each independent company is facing, and doing everything properly, from a senior shareholder's perception. It's important that there's a hierarchy and structure that allow independent companies to run independently, yet ensure that they are being monitored and are reporting on a regular basis, and are compliant with company policies."

"I've been here thirty-six years, and I admire a lot of my forefathers," adds Grieve. "There has been a tremendous effort over the years to write down how things are done properly. Policy, processes, and procedures are all recorded. We share it with new people, and are consistent across the organization. We want people to be able to walk into a new PCL environment and find consistency. Systems have been well developed and well documented. They work.

"A big part of structural and organizational success is having well-developed and effective communication systems throughout an organization. You must make sure that everybody who should know what's going on does know. There can't be surprises. If trouble surfaces, it needs to be identified and dealt with."

Risk mitigation is crucial in the construction trade, where growth is largely bid based. A company cannot grow by taking on jobs it cannot properly execute, on either a cost or a process basis. Getting it wrong not only loses the company money, it tarnishes its reputation in the trade and undermines its position when bidding on the next job.

"PCL is a textbook case of a company with good control systems," says Dimnik. "Most companies have diagnostic systems that tell managers if they are on track to achieving company goals, but it is a lot tougher to implement systems that question the goals themselves: are you doing the right thing in the right way? Formalizing organizational learning is very difficult, especially in large companies. PCL is a great example of a 'learning' company. Where most managers hide mistakes and so never learn from them, PCL management see mistakes as opportunities for learning. They succeed because they can learn from their mistakes."

"You try to learn from mistakes and not endure them more than once," says Grieve. "We've seen owners, banks, and subcontractors go broke. We've seen the good, the bad, and the ugly of the business. We've built protection into our processes, with very strict rules about the dos and don'ts of situations. It's only when we break rules that we get into trouble. We have a well-developed estimating and bid-closing system. Mistakes can be made when there's stress on people who are going at the max. But when you've got the forms and the checks and balances and the procedures, they can avoid errors. It's when you take shortcuts that Murphy's Law is waiting for you. We keep and teach the discipline."

The Deloitte perspective

Designing the right organization and processes to support growth

PCL has created an entrepreneurial culture throughout the organization largely due to the employee ownership, which is a key part of its core values. Its continuous improvement process, QUEST, is also critical to its success, providing the company with significant organizational value and a "can do" culture. QUEST initiatives lead PCL in the development of business strategy and practices, as well as overall corporate vision.

No matter how good its business strategy is, every company must periodically assess its organizational structure and processes, and then systematically plan for reorganization to support its current priorities. To evaluate whether your organization's structure is optimal for growth, keep in mind these features: the company's age and size, its stages of evolution, and the growth rate of its industry. The following provides a good summary of what to consider:

Identify the right organization structure and supporting processes for the company:

- In the start-up phase, construct an organization structure and processes to foster the entrepreneurial culture.
- During the formative phase, the organization structure and processes should deepen the functional expertise of the company.

- In the stabilization phase, the organization structure and processes should be conducive to balancing autonomy with efficiency.
- Finally, in the corporation phase, the organization structure and processes should enhance collaboration and teamwork.

Avoid the common pitfalls of reorganization efforts:

- Reduce unclear accountability by making sure there are no overlapping accountability and non-quantifiable objectives.
- Reduce unnecessary layers by examining, during the reorganization, every layer between the CEO and the lowest units in the organization to determine whether these layers are adding value.
- Identify and neutralize the negatively impacted stakeholders by changing their negative perceptions or reducing their influence.

Initiate the reorganization:

- Create buy-in at the top and initiate a systematic communication plan to influence the perceptions at all levels.
- Identify the compelling need to change and communicate the change effort to the organization.
- Identify, procure, and mobilize the necessary resources to support reorganization.

Commitment

9 Building a better circus

Creating the right leadership and communicating the vision

Cirque du Soleil

Canada's 50 Best Managed Companies winner, 1996

Many things bedazzle the visitor at Cirque du Soleil's headquarters in Montreal: the training and rehearsal studios, whose ceilings soar as high as any circus big top, the sprawling machine shop in which all the necessary hardware for acrobatic performances are custom made—even the circular red sandstone table in the reception area, almost mischievously suspended about a foot above the floor from wires secured to a ceiling several storeys high. But what especially bedazzles is the infrastructure devoted to costumes.

There is a fabric studio, where almost all the patterned or decorated cloth used in creating costumes for Cirque's numerous shows is custom silk-screened or hand-painted. Separate departments are dedicated to designing and making footwear, headwear, and bodysuits. A staff of three hundred is required to produce, maintain, and replace the costumes worn by the nearly eight hundred performers who are appearing in eleven permanent and touring Cirque du Soleil shows around the globe. There are three copies of every costume worn by a performer, and some performers may have more than one role in a given performance. That translates into anywhere from 3000 to 4200 costumes in existence at any time, all documented, all custom made to fit an individual performer.

Which brings us to the room full of heads. Costumes must fit individual performers, some of them flying through the air, others tumbling in water, with absolute precision, and headgear especially so. And so, when new performers join the company, they have their heads reproduced for the costume makers.

The head is encased in dental moulding material, which is then wrapped in plaster. The performer breathes through straws in his or her nose as the plaster sets, which takes about forty-five minutes. The finished mould produces remarkable detail, down to skin pores. The plaster head made from the mould is numbered, inventoried, and when not in use by a costume maker, stored on a shelf in a room just off the area where bolts of fabric are kept.

Cirque du Soleil never gets rid of these heads, even after a performer departs the company, which on average happens after he or she has been with it about four years. Twenty percent annual rollover is the figure Cirque works from in recruiting, auditioning, and training new performers. That creates an awful lot of heads. They number in the thousands now, lined up on the shelving. Even for Cirque employees, they are a continuing source of fascination. You can stare into this army of disembodied faces for ages. Male and female, they represent every race, creed, and colour of humanity, most of them young, but some of them (particularly the clowns) older and in middle age. To contemplate Cirque's heads is to appreciate the diversity of the human form. If a physical anthropologist ever learns of this room, there will be no end to the demands to access it.

It takes a while to put a finger on what is so especially compelling about the Cirque heads. The expressions are peaceful. The eyes and lips are closed; some of them are smiling. Finally, it hits you: these heads are *dreaming*.

Cirque du Soleil began as a dream of another possibility for circus arts, and has come to be widely celebrated for its dreamlike, otherworldly worlds. (Commentators searching for a description of its performances tend to settle on "ethereal.") With annual revenues of about U.S.$500 million and thirty-five hundred employees, it has become a dominant player in global entertainment because of its ability to infuse an organization that is continually growing (and changing in its participants) with a complex but coherent vision of precisely what Cirque is, and what it can be. That vision comes directly from its founders, one of whom, Guy Laliberté, is the majority owner of the privately held company and continues to serve as a guiding spirit and critical eye. The vision must be communicated to all who participate in creating Cirque's dreamlike worlds, and be respected as the bedrock of the company's operations.

Cirque today has six touring companies and five permanent shows (four in Las Vegas, one at Walt Disney World in Florida), with two more permanent shows in development (another for Las Vegas in 2006, one for Tokyo Disney Resort in 2008). The company is satisfied with juggling the logistics of six touring companies, and the business plan calls for three more permanent shows in the near future; the company is considering London, New York, and Paris. Factor in ancillary activities in television, music, and DVD, and the company seems very, very far removed from the sprightly band of street performers that first appeared under the Cirque du Soleil name in Quebec in 1984. But the present links seamlessly with the past, and it is the considerable responsibility of the executives who run Cirque today for Laliberté—mainly, president and chief operating officer Daniel Lamarre, and the chief financial officer, Robert Blain—to ensure that as Cirque continues to grow as an enterprise, that link is never broken.

Robert Blain left Deloitte to join Cirque du Soleil in 1994. About a year ago, Blain muses, Guy Laliberté asked him what had ever made him give up the security of Deloitte to literally run away and join the circus.

"First of all, it was the product," says Blain. "I was impressed by the show. Second, it had two leaders with vision who were entrepreneurs. Their focus was on the quality of the product. There were no compromises. And they respected the consultants they hired, paying the fees without question. They were always ready to work with the best people. And with them, there were no compromises on their personal values. They have principles, and they stick to them.

"The most important thing with Cirque du Soleil has been artistic control. The goal is to provoke, invoke, evoke emotions of people. A new show is a white page. It's part of Guy's mandate to find the right creative team. He doesn't ever say, 'This will be the show.'"

The creative process remains the foundation of Cirque. It was paramount to Laliberté at the inception, and remains so, even as Cirque has become a globe-girding multimillion-dollar venture. It doesn't invest in market research that's aimed at telling the developers of new shows what will sell best. Cirque's market research is more hands-on and exploratory. It works hard to stay abreast of cultural trends. A few years ago, Guy Caron, a long-standing artistic associate of Laliberté (and founder, in 1981, of the National Circus School, located next door to Cirque's Montreal headquarters) was sent travelling the globe for a year, to see what interesting things were brewing, culturally. Scouts who look for performing talent also keep eyes and ears peeled wherever they are for new sounds, new visual expressions. A new hotel interior, an obscure musical performer, is worthy of comment.

It sometimes seems easier to define what Cirque isn't than what it is. From the beginning, Cirque wanted to create an alternate circus, an anti-circus, even. To North Americans especially, the circus had a fairly predictable set of elements that hearkened back to the nineteenth century and were refined and institutionalized by established operations such as Ringling Bros. and Barnum & Bailey: clowns with red noses and little cars, performing animals (horses, elephants, big cats, the occasional seal), and high-wire acts. There were other components, but those were the main ones. Cirque began building its own version of the circus, working up and out from the ranks of street buskers: jugglers, stilt-walkers, fire-breathers, acrobats. Initially, it had something of a medieval–early Renaissance feel, of a May Day celebration gone sideways.

With time, the Cirque experience was refined, and its sophistication increased. The company kept setting the bar higher for itself, and still does. Certain things have remained outside the Cirque tent. There are no performing animals. There are no headline acts, because unlike a traditional circus, Cirque is not a disconnected series of performance set pieces. Each show has a theme, and performers are characters. Where the old circus lured audiences with the Fabulous Zucchini Brothers on their flying trapezes (and the modern Vegas transplant of the big cat show had Siegfried and Roy), Cirque has never had celebrity performers. It recruits acrobats from the world of competitive gymnastics, and many Cirque performers have been world-class athletes who represented their countries at Olympic Games, but Cirque has never attempted to build a showcase for an Olympic gold medalist. Cirque is as much a theatre or dance company as it is a circus, and even so, there are no marquee names, with Cirque neither recruiting them nor building individual performers into them.

Laliberté has followed the principle of not having headliners from the beginning. A cynic might point to the financial savings in not having star performers, but there is nothing inexpensive about the way a Cirque show is developed or mounted. And the policy has proved fundamental to the longevity of Cirque productions. Touring shows are designed to last for incredible runs of twelve to fifteen years, though they are regularly updated, and a creative director travels with them so as to be able to tweak them. Without the lengthy runs, the expense of developing and mounting the shows would not be feasible. *BusinessWeek* has noted that the total cost of creating *KÀ* for the MGM Grand in Las Vegas, at U.S.$165 million (which included building the theatre itself), eclipsed the production expense of all thirty-six shows on Broadway in 2004. Shows can run for such great lengths only if the performers, especially ones in demanding acrobatic roles, can regularly be replaced.

While Cirque is not beholden to any single performer, neither is it beholden to a particular style or presentation. The company faces a very tall order: to continue to be distinctively Cirque, without being predictable, repetitive. "I challenge anyone to tell me there are similarities between our Las Vegas shows," says Lamarre, a television and public relations executive hired to run Cirque in 2001. "The similarities are in *quality*." And with the fifth Las Vegas show in development, a secretive Beatles tribute production that may well bring to life in 2006 the hallucinatory world of the feature-length animation *Yellow Submarine,* the company clearly is headed in directions that are recognizably Cirque, but at the same time unrecognizable, based on any of its current shows. The Beatles production will not be *Corteo,* the newest touring show, which debuted in Montreal in April 2005, and *Corteo* was not *"O,"* the aquatic show that opened at the Bellagio hotel in Las Vegas in 1998. And certainly none is the erotically charged *Zumanity,* Cirque's reinvention of the cabaret for the New York, New York hotel and casino in Las Vegas in 2003.

The company is now widely imitated, or is at least a reference point for critics trying to put their fingers on the qualities of another venture's performance. (A case in point: the Cedar Lake Ensemble, a New York–based ballet company formed in 2002 by Wal-Mart heiress Nancy Walton, has been called "Cirque-like" in its multimedia approach to a particular touring production.) And it faces competition from within its own (former) ranks. Franco Dragone, who was synonymous with Cirque productions until the late 1990s, directing *Mystère* and *"O"* for Las Vegas hotels owned by Steve Wynn, left Cirque and created *Le Rêve* for Wynn's latest hotel, Wynn Las Vegas. Like *"O," Le Rêve* is water-based. Cirque du Soleil was compelled to add an FAQ page to its website, explaining that while Dragone did create both *"O"* and *Le Rêve,* Dragone no longer works for Cirque, *Le Rêve* is not a Cirque production, and no, you can't exchange tickets for one show to attend the other.

When you see shows that are said to be Cirque-like, you know they are not Cirque du Soleil. Cirque employees seem to have developed a highly intuitive feel for what their product is and isn't. "Take ten different employees and say, 'Is this Cirque?' and they will all have the same answer," says Lamarre. "You cannot *not* understand the artistic values of this organization. We defend the brand with our artistic values."

"A lot of it is intuitive," offers Renée-Claude Ménard, Cirque's public relations director. "People from Cirque know it. If something doesn't have a Cirque feel, the system will kick it out automatically. It's going to be waste-managed. There's a very good creative filter at work."

"Every single person there seems to know what Cirque is, and that's amazing," says Shawna O'Grady, associate professor and director of team facilitation at Queen's School of Business. She has seen Cirque's *"O"* in Las Vegas and was sufficiently charmed to want to see more. "People obviously know the brand as well, and that's why they can attract high-quality talent. Then they somehow, through training, are able to communicate their culture to those people, and get them to understand what is and isn't Cirque. The clarity of vision from the top on down is remarkable."

The roots of Cirque du Soleil date back to street performers, commune residents, and folk musicians who entwined in the Quebec counterculture scene of the 1970s. A young globe-trotting folk musician named Guy Laliberté, who played accordion and harmonica, busked through Europe in the late 1970s, along the way learning fire-breathing from Parisian street performers. After returning home in 1979, he hooked up with Gilles Ste-Croix; after Laliberté served as Ste-Croix's campaign manager as he ran federally on the satirical Rhinoceros Party ticket, they created together a company of stilt-walkers and other performers, Les Échassiers de Baie-Saint-Paul, which in 1981 was folded into a non-profit holding company, Ste-Croix's Le Club des talons hauts—the High Heels Club.

Out of Le Club des talons hauts came La Fête foraine, a street festival for the town of Baie-Saint-Paul, near Quebec City.

Debuting in 1982, it ran for three successive summers under the direction of Laliberté. It provided the gestation of Cirque du Soleil.

For all its minstrelsy and counterculture roots, La Fête foraine demonstrated Laliberté's business acumen. After a small loss in the first year (when admission was free), the festival was profitable. "I had a business goal, always," Laliberté says in *Cirque du Soleil: 20 Years Under the Sun,* the company's twenty-year commemorative book published in 2004. "I knew it took discipline to make things happen, even when I did projects at school. I think it's a quality I have: I'm capable of finding a balance between business and creativity, and seeing how creativity can grow out of that balance."

The Baie-Saint-Paul entrepreneurs then caught wind of a major public event on the near horizon, the 450th anniversary, in 1984, of Jacques Cartier's first voyage to Canada. The Quebec government needed events and activities, and Laliberté thought he could supply one: a new circus, drawing on both local and international performers who were already participating in La Fête foraine. Lying on a beach in Hawaii, watching the sun go down, Laliberté came up with the name for the new troupe: Le Cirque du Soleil. On June 16, 1984, the age of the Circus of the Sun officially dawned. With a yellow and blue big top that could accommodate eight hundred spectators, Cirque opened in Gaspé and toured through ten other locations in the province.

It was supposed to be a one-off exercise, one of several projects under the umbrella of Le Club des talons hauts, but Cirque du Soleil found further reason for existence as the provincial and federal governments agreed to support the troupe for another tour in 1985, in concert with the UN's International Youth Year. Government grants in one form or another were part of Cirque's funding until about 1992, when the troupe became completely self-sufficient. That was when its oldest surviving touring show,

Saltimbanco, was born. *Alegría* followed in 1994, *Quidam* in 1996, *Dralion* in 1999, *Varekai* in 2002, and *Corteo* in 2005.

At the same time, Cirque was developing permanent shows for tourism destinations. The standard arrangement has been for Cirque's partner to create the required theatre. Cirque provides the show, and the two split the revenues. The first permanent show was *Mystère,* which opened at Treasure Island in Las Vegas in 1993. The City That Never Sleeps has proved to be a second home for Cirque: in addition to *"O"* and *Zumanity*, Cirque opened *KÀ* at the MGM Grand in 2004, and will deliver the Beatles show to the Mirage in 2006. Cirque's partnership with Disney began with *La Nouba* at Walt Disney World Resort in Orlando in 1998 and will continue with the Tokyo Disney Resort show in 2008.

By 1997, Cirque had grown to the point that it was operating out of sixteen locations around Montreal. Its 345,000-square-foot headquarters opened in the neighbourhood of St-Michel in 1997, which at first consisted of the studio training space, then doubled in size in 2001 with the opening of the Ateliers, where the costumes, props, and apparatus are produced. The interior design employs materials such as chipboard and sheet metal in an effort to evoke the street origins of the company. But a large Riopelle canvas, *La ligne d'eau,* hanging in the reception area, reminds the visitor that this is not a home to scrappy urchins.

Operating a company as large and sophisticated as Cirque required a five-year plan of target revenues and profits, but it did not create strict business plans for individual shows until complications arose with the development of the latest touring production, *Corteo.*

Since 2002, Cirque has been opening a new show every year. The process, notes Blain, has been a little different than that followed by other entertainment companies. As Blain explains, other companies would ask a creative team for its idea, and then tell it how much money it could have to execute it. Cirque instead would decide how much it could spend, and then expect the creative team to come up with their vision within its financial boundaries.

Cirque could rely on its track record to assess the costs involved in mounting a typical production. The company also understood its market very well, and knew the price points that Cirque could command for tickets. The company customarily would determine the size of the new show—typically, fifty to sixty performers are involved—and put together the creative team. A budget, usually about $25 million, would be set. "You would give them the envelope of money," explains Blain, "and say, 'You have to be in the envelope, and be ready on a particular day.'"

Corteo threw a spanner into the works when the creative team asked to reinvent the big-top experience of the touring show. Until then, Cirque's shows took place with the stage to one side of the tent and the support infrastructure behind it. But for *Corteo,* the creative team wanted rotating stages in the centre of the tent, with ramps leading out through either end and the "backstage" placed under the stage. It was essential, the team said, to the storyline. It would also increase the intimacy of the tent experience, because the audience would be in the round, and could see other members. But it was also going to cost $2.4 million more than what had been placed in the envelope.

"So we did a business plan," says Blain. "We did a five-year plan for the show, based on seating, price, and marketing. When we did the business case, the return was there." One of the influencing factors was that the new arrangement would increase the seating capacity from 2500 to 2680. The *Corteo* creative team got the extra money, and Cirque du Soleil was now producing business plans.

Which is not to say that, before then, Cirque was un-businesslike. In fact, it has been one of the most complex businesses imaginable.

Six touring companies alone, moving through North America, Europe, Asia, and Australia, mean a host of legal, financial, logistical, and human resources concerns, and the additional permanent shows only further complicate the corporate picture. With the touring shows, says Blain, "there is the whole aspect of putting up the tent, tearing it down, and putting the grass back"—the basic stuff of a circus that comes to town and hangs around for two months. Children touring with their families must be educated. "We're a local retailer in every city we visit," says Lamarre, "but a global company."

As Blain observes of the touring shows, "It's highly unusual for a company to build, hire, and then move every two months." And not just move, but move to different countries, which means revenues are coming in a stream of currencies whose exact mix changes as the tours shift countries and continents. Blain begins each day with a glance at currency exchange quotes. And travelling with these shows are teams of performers and support staff from around the world. "We have twenty-five different tax residences," Blain says of the payroll, "being paid in different currencies. Our payroll is more complex than Exxon's." Cirque began an overhaul of the payroll system in 2004, and it expects that it will take until about 2008 to get it the way Cirque wants it. Blain explains that Cirque has to develop its own payroll system because outside contractors were too daunted by the task.

If the direction of Cirque du Soleil were left to finance people from the world of large corporations, a few aspects would unquestionably change. It would more than likely ease out of the touring company trade, since the costs and complexities are so much higher than with the permanent shows. And you would probably see pressure to cut back on the international nature of the company, if only to get rid of the payroll headaches and taxation complexities.

That Cirque has not done this illustrates how well its management understands the core factors in its continued success. Cirque was born as a touring company, under the big top, or *grand chapiteau.* The touring shows are part of its soul and will not be abandoned. But a business case can still be made for them: they take the Cirque product to markets where no permanent show can ever be established, and they are an important factor in risk management. Tours are planned three to five years in advance, with more detailed planning occurring over a twelve- to eighteen-month period, with ticket sales beginning eight to nine months before a show arrives. Should there be some problem with a particular market, the tour can be adjusted. And having shows that are constantly on the move offsets the risk factors Cirque is now exposed to in Las Vegas, where some kind of catastrophe could shut down revenues from what will soon be five permanent shows on the casino strip.

As for the international composition of its casts, support employees, and creative teams, whatever the payroll problems it creates, this mix has been critical to Cirque's ability to create shows that transcend most cultural barriers. Very little in any touring show is adjusted for local markets. "We force creative teams," says Lamarre. "We compose them from different nationalities. At the beginning there is a clash, because they're from different cultures, but we say, 'We're sorry, but you have to work together.' Usually, other circuses have a particular national character. Cirque du Soleil is the only international brand, and it gives us a huge edge. The best people want to work with us, especially people who are reluctant to work with a multinational corporation. They know the facilities we have, and that the head of the company is an artist himself."

Preserving the special character of Cirque was a major consideration when co-owner Daniel Gauthier, who had been Laliberté's business partner since 1987 (and had known him since high school), decided to move on in 2001. "We had to buy back his 50 percent of the company," says Blain. "A lot of people were saying, 'Go public, you'll have all that cash.' The challenge was to keep the company private. Guy said no to going public. 'Find the money. I want to focus on creating shows, not on quarterly results.' It was the right decision, but it was tough. We borrowed the funds, but three times we have renegotiated credit facilities on better terms."

The decision not to go public proved beneficial when the company decided not to proceed with a new initiative, Complex Cirque. The idea was to extend Cirque's creativity to an all-encompassing destination that would include a hotel, boutiques, and a theatre. The first was to be built in Montreal, but the concept was judged to be too risky. "We didn't have to go back to the markets and say we'd changed our mind," says Blain. "And I have more time to put into development, and not be worrying about share price."

"Guy Laliberté has kept the company private and has hired a really strong leadership team that works closely, and with everyone else, together in the same building," says O'Grady. "He can focus on what he's doing, and others focus on the systems to manage the growth. The risk as the company gets bigger is: Can they replicate that working relationship in another management team, and another set of players?" The team that is in place now seems to be clicking nicely. "If the CFO was too different from Laliberté, they couldn't work with someone so creative at the top," says O'Grady. "The strengths of the executives are different from his own, but they aren't far off his own passion. They're people who have a passion themselves for the company. They all get it."

Keeping all these shows going, and adding another new show every year, has placed tremendous demands on Cirque in attracting and retaining talent. The demanding nature of acrobatics (and the personal strains of being on the road) means that Cirque performers, as noted, typically remain for about four years, although some have lasted a decade or more, particularly in the case of less physically demanding roles such as musicians. Cirque has programs that encourage performers who are ready to step off the stage to move into other areas of the business, from coaching to rigging to the costume department to some sort of white-collar job. But the company has also had a human resources staffer make the shift to performing, becoming a character in *Mystère.*

Finding and training new performers is a particular Cirque talent. A dozen scouts are on the lookout for prospects around the globe, and the company maintains a database of twenty thousand artists. About 70 percent of recruits come from a sports background, specifically gymnastics. They have the discipline and technical skills: what they usually lack is acrobatic and artistic training. Since opening the new headquarters, Cirque has held an annual training session, to which the most promising prospects are invited. For many, it is a major adjustment: not only are they in a different country but they are shifting into a world of expression. There are no more micromanaged routines with stern judges watching for the slightest variations from the deemed norm.

A new class under way in a Cirque headquarters studio in May 2005 provides a first-hand glimpse of the retraining that must occur. Recruits begin with the *jeux* class, which is about games, or role-playing, not training for any particular role in any particular show. "Week one is very hard," says publicist Chantal Côté, as she guides our visit through the headquarters. This year, changes were made to the studio, in seemingly subtle things like lighting, to make it feel less like a gymnasium, to deliberately move the recruits out of their old athletic environment. "At the introduction, they're told they will deal with uncertainty, ambiguity. What's fantastic about it is to watch them progress. They're much more aware of how they can use their body to express themselves."

"Imagine the kind of person who is attracted to that kind of working environment," O'Grady proposes of Cirque du Soleil in general, and not just these artistic recruits. "It takes special people who rise to the pressures and challenges. A lot of companies hire good people and then let them sink or swim. Cirque is hiring people and inculcating them in the culture. The high quality in talent, in everything they do, is key. It shows through the training and high expectations they set."

A young man, whose previous life involved strict gymnastic routines, is making a high-pitched buzzing noise in the *jeux* class. He appears to be imitating an insect. It's difficult to say. But he's having a great time doing it. And the performance sure isn't something you'll encounter as a required element in a floor routine at the Olympics.

In 1999, with Cirque having moved in a new performance direction with the aquatic show *"O"* in 1998, and a new touring show, *Dralion,* opening, the company wrapped up a strategic planning process which concluded that the company would become brand-driven. Coincidentally, Cirque was experiencing internal disquiet over its new show, *Dralion,* which drew heavily on Chinese performing talents and motifs. *Dralion* was the culmination of Laliberté's fascination with Chinese performers that dated back to an awe-inspiring visit by the Circus of China to Montreal in 1982, and Laliberté's 1986 trip to China. But *Dralion* was also the first production to follow the departure of Cirque's long-standing director Franco Dragone. As *Dralion*'s artistic director, Sylvie Galarneau, reflects in *Cirque du Soleil: 20 Years Under the Sun,* "Somehow, what we did was too big of a change for a lot of people within Cirque to digest. We thought: 'My God, what have we done?'"

As it turned out, *Dralion* became Cirque's most successful touring show to date. And having decided to become brand driven, Cirque had to define its brand. And to define its brand, it needed a brand manager, which it had never had on staff. In January 2000, Joanne Fillion left Molson Inc. across town to join Cirque as senior brand manager. It was a huge (and welcome) change for her from the focus-group-driven marketing of beer.

"The first thing I did at Cirque was realize that Guy Laliberté was in fact the brand manager," she says. "Not officially, but he was. It was his vision. He was giving yea or nay to projects, to advertising campaigns.... But if the company got bigger, he wouldn't be able to keep handling every single thing." In a way, Fillion was charged with making a cast of Laliberté's head, so that anyone working on any aspect of Cirque could ensure that what they were doing was form-fitted to it.

"I first tried to understand what the brand meant internally, to people who worked at Cirque," she says. "But a brand doesn't live internally—it lives outside. I began to conduct a brand audit internationally, to understand what it meant all over the world." When Fillion was finished her branding exercise, in 2001 (although she says the brand identity is a constant work in progress), the results reflected with remarkable fidelity what Laliberté had been espousing for years, but which had never been set down in stone ... or cast in plaster.

Cirque knew it had to get something down on paper, to define itself for its own sake. The company was growing quickly, and there had to be a consistent vision that everyone involved with the creation and promotion of Cirque shows understood. "Because of our growth," says Renée-Claude Ménard, "we have to be careful. We have new creative teams, new staff members. We have to keep them abreast of, 'This is who we are.'"

"I tried to institutionalize the brand, because of its impact on things such as potential projects and advertising campaigns," says Fillion. It would also guide the company in its search for brand extensions, opportunities that take Cirque beyond the circus-based performance.

Part of the reason for the branding exercise was succession planning. Although Laliberté was only forty years old in 1999 when he made the decision for Cirque to be brand-driven, the need to buy out Daniel Gauthier soon afterward made the brand definition crucial to the operations of the growing company. While Laliberté would remain very much involved in creative oversight, executives such as Blain and Lamarre would have to move the company forward, assess new business opportunities, and run Cirque in a way that recognizes its core values—because to protect them is to benefit from them. Another important factor is that Cirque relies on contracted, independent talents in creative areas. When a celebrated theatre director such as Robert Lepage is brought in to create a new show (as Lepage was, for *KÀ* in 2000), there have to be guiding principles, certain boundaries for the playing field. Lepage pushed those boundaries with *KÀ*. The show was more linear in its narrative than anything ever staged by Cirque, and had such novel elements as martial arts, puppetry, and pyrotechnics, but the process of creating *KÀ* still took place within the boundaries of the brand definition Cirque had determined for itself.

It's a highly qualitative brand definition, one that an acrobat can appreciate. You can perform all kinds of marvellous routines, but the equipment, the brand, has particular dimensions, much like the apparatus on which you're spinning and leaping.

It took Fillion and her team sixty-eight "values" to describe and define the Cirque brand. To make them more manageable, they were grouped into seven "pillars":

- *Creative-driven:* "If it's not creative, not new, not pushing the envelope, it's not Cirque," says Fillion. "Guy hates recipes; he's a risk taker and a visionary. Even if people are resisting change—saying, 'Hey, it's going well, why change?'—we will change. When another company copies something we did five years ago, and presents it today, well, we just did *KÀ,* and they'll have a hell of a job copying that one. It's in the DNA of this company that people are not taking no for an answer. They'll say, 'What do you mean it's not feasible? Let's put our heads together and work it out.'"
- *Human-centric:* "The human being is at the centre," says Fillion, "whether performing or producing, but also because the theme of everything is human-inspired. Cirque has universal emotions and subject matter."
- *Open architecture:* "We try to create shows or other products that give you the possibility for interpretation," says Fillion. "Even if *KÀ* is more linear in its story, Lepage will tell you there are four or five different levels on which you can read his creation. What makes Cirque so Cirque is that the viewers create their own story and make it very personal."
- *Emotion evoking:* "Cirque cannot be just visually beautiful," says Fillion. It must touch the viewers' hearts. Spectacle in and of itself is soulless.

- *Nomadic in spirit:* "People seeing Cirque as another world," says Fillion. "We've been travelling for twenty-one years now, and that has brought a flavour to what we do. No one sees Cirque as culture specific." Its shows don't have one particular culture's sound or look. "Cirque is a fusion of cultures and experiences."
- *Attention to detail and level of quality:* "The bar is very high in everything we do. If we're not up to par, we know that really fast. Expectations are very high."
- *Sensory abundance:* "When we do something, it's a sensory overload."

The brand definition is important to ensuring that shows as they are developed remain, however adventurously imagined and executed, definably "Cirque." It also gives the senior brand director a reference point for pursuing new business opportunities. The Cirque brand can be taken beyond the big top, and this is a particular ambition of the company at the moment: to seek out potential brand extensions, opportunities that do not involve the company's core product, the live, circus-based show.

Cirque's branding exercise means that Cirque is in control of its own brand, making its own decisions about the nature of its shows. It has partnerships with Disney for its permanent shows in Orlando and Tokyo, but that doesn't mean Cirque is having to fit Goofy, Winnie the Pooh, the Muppets, or any other Disney properties into the act. The new alliance to produce the Beatles show (struck with Paul McCartney, Ringo Starr, and the estates of John Lennon and George Harrison) is a distinct departure for Cirque, and until the final production is unveiled it is impossible to say how the worlds of Cirque and the Liverpool mop tops will merge. But the fantastical possibilities (particularly in *Yellow Submarine*) seem like a good fit, so much so that it's difficult to imagine who other than Cirque du

Soleil could do the Sea of Green proper justice. We'll know for certain when the long-legged gentlemen in top hats start dropping giant apples on the heads of the hapless residents of Pepperland.

The Beatles show is a perfect example of why it is so dangerous to try to define Cirque by what it doesn't do, because it will do things it hasn't done before, if it fits the brand definition. Such was the case with *Zumanity,* as there had been no nudity in any of Cirque's previous productions. "The real challenge is to understand the elasticity of the brand," says Fillion. "Even in the show category, we are pushing the envelope all the time. It's why, with *Zumanity,* we signalled to the consumer that this would be another side of Cirque du Soleil. It was another part of the Cirque brand platform." Ménard calls it "the dark side of Cirque."

And nobody went swimming in a Cirque production until *"O."* But while the Beatles show appears to be taking Cirque into a cartoon world already described by a film, that doesn't mean Cirque can be expected to produce a show about the Flintstones, or Bugs Bunny, or Mickey Mouse. The Beatles show is not a case of Cirque declaring, "Now we're in the live cartoon business." It's a case of taking advantage of a perfect match of sensibilities, especially given Cirque's roots in counterculture.

Cirque's attention to excellence and careful brand management has paid off not only at the box office but in accolades from business professionals. In both 2004 and 2005, subscribers to *Canadian Business* and *Marketing,* who were polled by marketing firm Strategic Council and branding agency Spencer Francey Peters, rated Cirque du Soleil among the top handful of the best-managed brands in Canada. In 2004, Cirque tied with the venerable *Hockey Night in Canada,* pulling ahead in 2005 when the lockout cancelled the NHL season. The vicissitudes of pro-sports labour relations aside, Cirque was a rarefied company in 2005, outpolled only by the far more ubiquitous consumer brands Tim Hortons and President's Choice, and ahead of WestJet and Canadian Tire. It was a striking performance by a company whose product is mostly consumed internationally, and reflected the high regard in which Cirque is held among marketing professionals.

But you can only do so much with a brand if its product isn't also a world-class market leader. Cirque's branding discipline provides a framework in which Guy Laliberté's vision can find profitable opportunities, but at the end of the day, the competitive edge of Cirque comes substantially from the hothouse of experiment and excellence it has created in its new Montreal headquarters. Reflecting on the palpable buzz of the facility, Lamarre offers: "What you're seeing is a unique, creative laboratory. Because of that, we have an edge. We have leadership in the industry."

"The challenge is how to maintain that spirit of creativity while you're growing," says Fillion. "So far we've been pretty good. The creators' list on *KÀ* was absolutely amazing. Because it was Cirque, they were willing to play with us for a while. But it's been written so many times that businesses that have been innovative have been stalled by the size of the machine. And we are completely aware of that."

The Cirque brand has been pushing beyond the touring big top, first to the permanent shows, then into other live and multimedia opportunities. It has a deal with Celebrity Cruise Lines for voyages that feature Cirque-created lounges and Cirque performers, and is branching out with a new live show focusing on music, which will appear in 2006.

Multimedia, particularly film and television, have been natural outgrowths for the company, both as products in their own right and as promotions for the greater Cirque brand. A television special on *Saltimbanco* won its producer, Télémagik Productions, a gold medal at the New York Festivals in 1995, and other awards in film and television for Cirque productions have followed, including a number of Emmy Awards, to go along with numerous prizes internationally for the company's live performances.

Particularly well received was *Cirque du Soleil Fire Within,* a reality series that captured performing candidates making it—and breaking it—in training. The ups and downs of one particular recruit, an English gymnast named Garrett Hopkins, kept viewers coming back. He ultimately washed out; and the unvarnished drama of his inability to make the transition from amateur gymnast to professional circus performer deserved much credit for the Emmy and Gemini wins that the series enjoyed in 2003.

While seated in the cafeteria, a visitor to Cirque's headquarters remarks to Renée-Claude Ménard on the irresistible narrative pull of Garrett's travails. She looks over the visitor's shoulder and brightly announces, "He's right behind you."

And he is. Garrett has come back, participating in a creative workshop for a new project in development, and he is standing in the cafeteria lineup with his fellow performers. A moment no one would dream to dream up.

The Deloitte perspective

Creating the right leadership and communicating the vision

The key to success with Cirque du Soleil is its creative mindset, its capacity to always think outside the box, which is an integral part of its business culture. The company's sense of innovation is witnessed primarily in the artistic and mechanical components of the shows but can also be found in all aspects of the business.

Cirque is also better than most other enterprises at building excellent relationships with its business partners. It manages to achieve a strong sense of belonging among its employees, but also does so among its business partners in general. To achieve that sense of belonging, Cirque invites these partners regularly to events such as show premieres, private parties, and golf tournaments. Even where the clients are the general public, they strive to achieve a similar sense of belonging.

Unquestionably, it was Guy Laliberté's values, allied with his vision of what Cirque du Soleil could become, that spawned its phenomenal success. As with all great leaders, Laliberté quickly realized he needed his employees—especially the leaders of the company—to support his vision and accept the new values he was inculcating in Cirque.

The company brings excitement to all levels of employees. It minimizes formalities in order to focus on the content of each task, each relationship, and each individual. They are informal in their dress code, office layout, and interpersonal relationships. When hiring people, expertise, experience, and competencies are important selection criteria, but they attach as much importance to the fit with the culture of the organization, the interpersonal skills, and the team-playing orientation of the candidates.

The lessons to be drawn from the success of Cirque can be easily overlooked, as it may not seem that the goals, practices, and processes of a hyper-creative entertainment phenomenon have much relevance in less exotic corporate environments. Nevertheless, Laliberté cultivated a vision for Cirque and designed a leadership structure found within all levels of the organization, which follows the sound and proven approach outlined below, and which can be generalized to apply to most companies, with or without trapeze artists on their payrolls:

Recognize the organization's requirements:

- Determine what the organization's leadership needs are in order for them to achieve the company's objectives.
- Determine the leadership team's roles and responsibilities.
- Match the company needs to the current organization and identify the areas for improvement.

Make the company's leaders more effective:

- Recognize the roles the company's leaders must play in order to address the organization's business challenges.
- Ensure the chosen leadership style is appropriate, given the external and internal climates.
- Ensure all the leaders follow a similar leadership process and communicate the same vision.

Develop the leadership team:

- Assess employees using a performance measurement process that allows the organization to identify its potential future leaders.
- Create a development process—including mentoring, coaching, and discussing—that will help the selected candidates develop their leadership skills.
- Foster a leadership culture through the entire company that will continuously generate leaders at all levels.

Often, with outstanding corporate success stories such as Cirque, it is the drive and ambition, the vision and genius, of one or two people that create the company. But it is only with the addition of leaders who share and can communicate core values that sustained growth can be achieved. This also enables the company to make faster and more effective decisions, enhances understanding of the company's brand, strengthens cohesion among its employees, and, finally, provides greater flexibility in adopting—or, in Cirque's case, creating—market changes.

10 Hire learning

Attracting and retaining talent to build an exceptional culture

National Leasing

Canada's 50 Best Managed Companies winner, 1994–2002
Named to Platinum Club, 2003

Human resources departments are famous for explaining to fresh-scrubbed recruits how many years of service they must log before the golden handshake of retirement is extended their way. The response of a twentysomething coming out of university or college can be a hundred-mile stare, as this newcomer to full-time employment boggles at the actuarial calculation presented to them by the HR professional.

Not everyone showing up for his or her first job relishes the thought of spending an entire career with the same business. Even so, the last thing new hires expect to hear from an employer is the alternative—that they shouldn't expect to stay with this company for their entire working lives. Companies that claim to engender employee-focused cultures as a rule don't tell young and eager recruits that they already should be thinking about moving on. Yet National Leasing's disarmingly frank approach could be summed up with the greeting "Welcome aboard. Be prepared to leave."

About a dozen years ago, president and CEO Nick Logan began telling his staff that National Leasing could not be considered their "employer for life." As he observes, "That didn't go over well at the time. In fact, colleagues said to me, 'You can't tell people that they'll be let go.'" But that wasn't what Logan was saying—and continues to say. He expects that people who come to work for National Leasing want challenges, want to see progress in their careers. The day they stop seeing progress for themselves at National Leasing is the day they should be prepared to take their skills elsewhere.

And the relationship cuts both ways. If National Leasing wants to attract the best employees, and hang on to them, it has to continually challenge them, train them, make their working lives fulfilling, give them opportunities to grow. The day those challenges are no longer available to them is the day those employees will move on. Nick Logan is prepared to accept that—and he needs employees who will accept it, too. He naturally wants people to stay with him, but he also wants them to know that it's his intention to make National Leasing a bright spot on their resumé. Come work for me, he has effectively said, and I will make you a headhunter's dream. Not the usual pitch you hear at a corporate recruitment session.

Headquartered in Winnipeg, National Leasing is Canada's largest lessor in small- to medium-sized equipment. It coalesced in 1987 from a group of diverse businesses being run by Nick Logan and others who would become part of National Leasing's senior management. There were ten enterprises in all. One of the businesses they shed was in automotive leasing. They kept a small-ticket business equipment leasing operation, and put it together with a software development company. The software expertise proved critical. The small-ticket leasing business proved phenomenally successful.

Just about any capital asset can be leased rather than purchased—and they are. Leasing has been embraced as an alternative to cash purchase or conventional financing by businesses and consumers alike. The total leasing market in Canada was estimated by the Canadian Finance and Leasing Association (CFLA) in 2004 to involve assets in the neighbourhood of $100 billion. And of the $84.5 billion Statistics Canada was predicting in machinery and equipment investments for 2004, CFLA estimated that between 20 and 25 percent of that value would take the form of leases—a significant jump from the less than 5 percent circa 1990.

The leasing industry has been distilling into two main camps: major enterprises affiliated with the manufacturers of the assets they lease, such as Ford Credit, GMAC, and Xerox Leasing; and niche players that have carved out specialty sectors of the economy, with almost no medium-sized operations in the space between them. National Leasing is one of the niche specialists, active in North America in health care, construction, agriculture, manufacturing, computer technology, and office interiors. Sales were about Can$180 million in 2003, an 18 percent improvement over the previous two years. It reviews about four thousand lease applications every month, and annually finances about $300 million worth of assets (about one-quarter of which is syndicated out), represented by some forty-five thousand lease agreements from clients in North America. Those assets may be dwarfed by the estimated $100 billion in total leased assets in Canada alone, but National Leasing nevertheless is considered an industry leader in small-ticket asset leasing. And the tickets have been getting bigger.

Leasing activity has grown by leaps and bounds since the first independent leasing operation appeared in the United States in 1952. Worldwide, annual plant and equipment leasing volumes (not including cars and trucks) grew from an estimated U.S.$40 billion in 1978 to about U.S.$479 billion by 1999. The appeal of leasing by now is well understood. It doesn't tie up capital in outright purchases, doesn't require additional assets to serve as collateral for loans, and the approval process uses a leasing industry creation, called cash flow–based credit analysis, rather than a traditional credit history. Monthly leasing costs are aligned with revenues and may offer tax advantages.

But in the 1990s, leasing became almost too much of a good thing, at least for the leasing industry. Even the CFLA has described the behaviour of some of its members in that decade as "freewheeling." Lease approval rates were high, generally above 70 percent, risk analysis wasn't always what it could have been, and, at times, the leasing industry's growth produced at the end of leases a surfeit of perfectly good second-hand assets that had to be disposed of, thus undercutting new lease opportunities. Lease companies were confronting a maturing industry with far less opportunity for robust revenue increases.

National Leasing enjoyed growth rates of 30 to 35 percent through the 1990s. Y2K helped slow down National's growth pace, but it still enjoyed an increase of 19 percent in 2004. Y2K also nudged the company toward a strategy of choosing niche markets in which it would specialize and develop a marketable expertise. It has targeted three specific market opportunities, which National defines as Golf and Turf, Medical/Dental, and Agriculture. The strategy has kept the business growing while increasing the average ticket size of lease items to more than $11,000.

The diversity of its leasing activities has made for one of the most eccentric collections of equipment and machinery under one corporate roof. Peruse National's clientele, and you will find them leasing dental X-ray machines, hay bale processors ("square and round, new and used"), veterinary ultrasound devices, telephone systems, auto-shop equipment, golf-course beverage carts, office photocopiers, industrial machine tools, computers, office furniture, and fertilizer bins (granular and liquid). It also expanded its product line in 2003 into life, disability, and critical-illness coverage for lessees on their lease payments, known as the Value Plus Program, through a referral partnership with the Sawka Group.

National Leasing says that its investment in technology has been second only to its investment in its sales organization. It has become notably internet savvy, deploying new software used both internally by staff and externally by customers. It redeveloped its accounts receivable software in-house in 2003, placing it in a web environment to improve collection, customer service, accounting, and asset management. Invoices and statements could shift over to faxes and email, reducing processing costs. The system has allowed National Leasing to increase business volume without adding staff, and its reporting capabilities provide better information for assessing credit worthiness and exposure levels on customer accounts. (National Leasing reports that thirty-day delinquency improved 95 percent in a single year, and its total delinquency was reduced to less than 1 percent of net investment in a lease, which it says compares well to U.S. industry averages of 3 to 6 percent).

The company also launched a Securitization Administration System in September 2002, developed in-house to automate the administration of the company's securitization portfolio. The result was a system that handles about 95 percent of all decision making, requiring little human intervention, while reducing administration costs. In June 2003, the U.S.–based Equipment Leasing Association awarded the company its Business Technology Solutions Award for the new system.

The list of technology innovations continues, but the main thing to take away from National Leasing's impressive growth is its overarching embrace of "high-performance management," the philosophy that gathered steam in the late 1990s and has picked up where "total quality management" (TQM) left off. Logan offers his own definition of high-performance management: "It is setting mutually dependent goals for both management and the organization and, of course, striving for some measured success or team batting average."

As applied by executives such as Logan, high-performance management has softened up the bureaucratic, process-obsessed bent of its predecessor, TQM, with "soft" human resources factors. Especially in the case of National Leasing, high-performance management embraces corporate culture as a competitive advantage.

Logan thinks most companies, and academics concerned with management theory, have been neglecting the importance of corporate culture, but he feels that awareness of it is improving and that it will, eventually, be more widely recognized as "an untapped asset." Before that happens, he says, top executives are going to have to understand the concept before a beneficial culture can be developed in a particular organization. "Research makes it clear that even during an economic downturn, companies with strong adaptive cultures perform significantly better, financially, than those with a weak or poorly defined culture," he avows.

In Logan's mind, "Culture drives the organization and its actions. It is akin to the operating system of the organization. It guides how employees think, act, and feel. It is dynamic and fluid, and never static. A culture may be effective at one time under a given set of circumstances and ineffective at another time. There is no generically 'good' culture."

The challenge in prioritizing culture as a competitive tool, Logan says, is that "the right culture for a company has no direct or obvious connection with performance. This can be an absolute mind-bender for linear thinkers." Management system expert Karen Legge, who is based in the United States, has called the quest to make a connection between profitability and high-performance management methods the Holy Grail of human resources management research.

Reduce borrowing costs, trim overheads, introduce a new product line, improve inventory turnover ... there are any number of things that a company can do to which a hard dollar value can be attributed on an income statement or balance sheet. "Culture" in and of itself doesn't show up anywhere. It's an intangible that can't be assigned a value. Improving it doesn't produce a beneficial change in the ratio of assets to liabilities. Business theorists, Logan feels, are frustrated by an inability to measure it. And when many CEOs cannot visualize the role and the impact of corporate culture, he notes, it becomes easy for their CFOs to block efforts to prioritize it.

In an organization that hires well to begin with, that is able to attract top people at whatever stage of its evolution, staff members are assets, best described as human capital. They might never appear on a balance sheet but rank in value on par with patents and other intellectual properties, and well ahead of wasting assets such as buildings, furniture, and delivery trucks. Every business can buy the same desktop computer off the shelf—or lease it from National. Not every business can attract, develop, and retain the same quality of talent. Human resources is one of the least appreciated creative enterprises. The right people must be found and, once aboard, given the opportunity to flourish, to grow, to the good of the company. And when employees recognize that what's good for the company is also good for them, regardless of whether or not they spend their entire careers with that company, their employer has fostered a corporate culture that is capable of reaching peaks of productivity and profitability.

And while "good culture" may not be a line item in the financials, the consequences of "bad culture" show up all over the place. It has a way of blowing through financial statements like shrapnel, causing all sorts of collateral damage.

Consider high recruitment costs—you have to work extra hard to convince people to work for you when informed and capable people would prefer not to, or when departures create an overload of candidate searching and interviewing. With high employee turnover, you're always on the recruiting treadmill. The ones you do persuade to work for you aren't the cream of the crop. The good ones you do fool into working for you leave at the earliest opportunity. If you've devoted any funds to employee training, it's been wasted if the employees keep walking out, taking enhanced skills elsewhere, especially to competitors. Many of the ones who choose to stay are the ones you rather had left. They're looking for long-term security, not challenges. Corporate culture becomes one of survival, of entrenched infighting, not of innovation or ambition. You're faced with high absenteeism, low productivity. The relationship between management and employees becomes one of mutual distrust, each side determined to deliver the bare minimum of their obligations to each other.

"They're doing very well in attracting and developing talent," says Shawna O'Grady, associate professor and director of team facilitation at Queen's School of Business. "They've got a great employer value proposition. A lot of employers are not defining well why you should work for their company. There's no brand essence. Nick Logan is pretty clear about what National Leasing is, and what it isn't. He is able to attract people to the organization, because it's very clear you'll get great training and have a great experience. The training aspect is key to the younger demographic in particular. A lot of companies are afraid to invest in employee training because employees might then leave for another company. When they say to me, 'What if I train them and they leave?' I say, 'What if you don't and they stay?'"

In all case studies of companies that have adopted high-performance management, those that excel do so by treating employees as an asset rather than as a bottom-line liability. They achieve growth and profitability sometimes by operating contrary to the status quo of their industry. Businesses that supposedly can compete only through low-cost labour have found success by exceeding industry wage standards and investing in their workforces. They also tend to have high training budgets, a reflection of their commitment to constant skills development.

They also tend, like National Leasing, to develop a reputation for being not only personally fulfilling and rewarding but also a fun place to work. (Listen to CEOs who embrace high-performance management and see how many mention "sense of humour" as an asset for candidates in executive recruitment.) National Leasing's list of employee amenities can make it sound more like a resort than a financial services enterprise. There are pool tables, an exercise room, and a "quiet room." It even owns a beachfront company cottage at Lake Winnipegosis, with a golf course out back. In the summer, three weeks out of four, it is available to employees, with the fourth week reserved for company hospitality. "It's a phenomenal treat for young employees to be able to take their family, their parents to it," says Logan. "They can say, 'Look what my company did for me.' It's not a party-animal retreat. It's a family chill-out centre."

Company-sponsored activities include Friday hockey, and pilates and yoga classes in the head-office recreation area. Every January, the company holds an "Olympic Games," in which employees organize into national teams and compete for gold medals in ping-pong, darts, billiards, and other such endeavours. Not only does it give Winnipeggers something to do in the depths of winter, it allows employees who otherwise wouldn't know each other to become better acquainted.

Doubtless for many corporate types, the sort of carryings-on this suggests is cringe inducing. How many of those dot.com start-ups had basketball half courts in the work area, in which young impresarios played some three-on-three pickup while burning through their venture capital? Indeed, as Logan admits, if all you had to go on was National Leasing's list of activities and amenities, "you might think we were pretty much off the wall. 'When do you work?' people ask me. The truth is that we are probably one of the more conservative companies around."

The leasing business is no place for a round-the-clock frat party. Logan observes that National Leasing has lost sixteen major competitors in the last ten years. "National has high standards. We are an industry leader, and an award-winning leader across the North American industry in technology. We have multiple sales distribution channels, and administration processes with an efficiency ratio comparable to the best financial service providers.

"We don't fool around when it comes to competitiveness. We fight for every deal like it is the only one out there. We have a strong balance sheet, our expenses are in line, and we produce 'top of the North American industry' earnings. Somehow the work gets done."

Logan firmly believes that "business can and should be fun. At far too many companies, you put on a mask when you come into the office. You look differently, talk differently, act differently than you do in real life. Unfortunately, so many business encounters are impersonal. At National, we try to create an environment where people can be themselves, not one where they are intimidated into controlled behaviour.

"We have the expectation that talented people will perform at a high level, given the proper supportive surroundings. Certainly it means frequent and open communication between a supervisor and the individual. There is regular feedback and monitoring of the individual's position within the life cycle of their current job responsibilities. When we expect a lot from people, we also recognize that to be well organized and focused also assumes that the same individuals have the same control over their personal issues."

Logan says a company needs to demonstrate flexibility in allowing employees to strike the necessary balance between work and private life. "This might mean something different to each person. It could mean flexible hours of work, a gymnasium in the office to make workouts convenient, work-from-home capabilities, lifestyle education delivered on a regular basis, or simply the ability to get personal things done during the day. Most enjoy their work, so when you allow them to satisfy the personal side, it releases them to excel on the professional side."

"To retain people," O'Grady advises, "you need to look at why employees stay, and also why they go. The number one reason employees leave is they don't have a good relationship with their boss. The main reason they stay is they feel well integrated or connected to the organization. There needs to be a good fit between their personal and professional lives."

O'Grady says that there are three fundamental strategies for attracting and then retaining top talent. First, "Create links to other people at work so they feel a sense of community. Use mentors and coaches. Creating links to the outside community can also be effective. National Leasing is managing the work-life balance very well."

Second, as employees move through their careers, ensure there is a proper passion for, and fit for, the job itself. The employees may be "entrenched," but they should also be highly motivated and productive.

And finally, "Create sacrifices, things which, if they left, they would have to give up. Training and development are some, perks are others." It comes back to the work-life balance. Companies such as National Leasing go beyond the basic paycheque in what they provide to the employee, and not all of what they provide has an absolute dollar value. Ultimately, employee loyalty can come down to a love of the corporate culture.

Logan advises that the process of creating a positive corporate culture begins with knowing what kind of culture you have, which is not, to him, a given. A company then needs to determine what the appropriate culture is—because culture is not a one-size-fits-all for organizations. What works for a ski resort isn't necessarily going to work for a diamond mine. And once the appropriate culture is determined, the company has to go about creating it. And that requires more than inspirational posters in the lunchroom. It also takes time—years, in fact. As Logan likes to point out, it took National Leasing three years just to build the company's cottage.

Logan is not a strong believer in overnight turnarounds, though he is well aware of our popular culture's fixation with extreme makeovers, with solutions in a box that can be unpacked, plugged in, and admired as it works transformative magic. "What happens when we realize that the problems are bad enough that they need fixing?" he proposes. "We rush around in a panic, looking to spend money on a quick fix. It's a consultant's dream account. People want 'new' and 'fast.' That's why the Atkins Diet is so popular. There is hope it will make up for a fundamentally unhealthy lifestyle. Unfortunately, crisis-driven change is usually not sustainable.

"Some organizations try to achieve high performance with quick fixes, such as a fast hire of a strong salesperson, and expect them to fit in and solve their revenue problems. Another quick fix is to fire the coach and bring up the next one, looking for changes. Many larger organizations look to consultants not familiar with their business for direction. For us, building a culture is a long-term drive to build an environment in which successful people can thrive, where their surrounds will change to support a combination of individual and corporate goals. We are committed to Winnipeg, the industry, and to growing organically. So we are not distracted by suitors or making significant acquisitions."

Logan argues that most great companies, brands, and careers have been forged the same way: "Bit by bit, step by step, inch by inch. The truth is that gradual change is challenging and hard. Challenging, because the people around you are demanding something right now. Hard, because gradual change requires the faith to know that your hard work is worth the investment."

Nick Logan calls leaders "inspirational role models who map out the route to a successful existence for the organization. Leaders do four things. They lead by example, they plan, they sort for quality, and they communicate."

And Logan cannot imagine anyone successfully implementing a high-performance management system, with a strong corporate culture at its core, if the company is losing money. "I remember two years where I was awash in red ink," he likes to relate. "The first was in grade eight, when I brought home my winter report card with most of my marks circled in red. My mother wouldn't sign it. The next time was in 1980–81, when the western [Canadian] economy crashed. I was living in Edmonton at the moment when the music stopped—you know the game, when there are not enough chairs. There was not enough money for those claiming it, sitting or standing. Those two vivid memories drive me personally not to go there again. I have to be profitable. That's my first premise."

For leadership to be effective, "success has to be attainable. Failure cannot be an option. With profits, you are able to take chances and make mistakes. You can't be afraid of making some gambles and losing. If you are afraid to swing for fear of missing the ball and losing a game, then there is no confidence. Without confidence, you can't win. That's a defensive culture, not a constructive one.

"People like to work for a winner, and they take pride in the competitive spirit required to maintain the number one position," he adds. "High-performance individuals insist on improving themselves and their surroundings. Managers facilitate that creativity."

In the pursuit of profitability, National Leasing relies on rolling forecasts, reviewed on a quarterly basis and approved by its board, to continually monitor management's twelve-month forward projections. Senior managers "are paid to create forecasts that generate an ROE [return on equity] in excess of a minimum standard. Think about that. I am not paying on results: I am paying for the plan to *get* the results. With approximately 40 percent of their compensation on the line every three months, there is a real incentive to develop the right plan. I would say that we have chosen to operate in the future to maximize our chances for success."

"Expectation-setting is key," says O'Grady. "People rise to a level set for them. Even if employees or their company don't reach the goals they set, people who have goals always outperform those who don't. If you aim at nothing, you can be sure you'll reach it."

Logan is also adamant that an organization's leadership cannot just hit rolling ROE targets but must also provide a positive role model for those they are expected to lead. That means not only recognizing positive performances but dealing unflinchingly with negative ones.

He wonders how often people think beyond the inappropriate individual behaviour that inevitably crops up in an organization, following the trail of culpability to the offender's supervisor, "where the source of the behaviour either started or is supported. If you come across a dishonest organization, chances are that it percolates down from the top—or, at best, there is some laziness within the leadership ranks. High performers expect leaders to deal with non-performers. Remember that people will hold you accountable for what you *can* do but choose not to do."

Logan believes that strong leaders and effective managers "set the stage in an organization with their personal values." The job of the CEO, and those who directly support him or her, "is to make sure you approve of the value system of every vice-president, senior manager, and as far down as you can go. If there is an inconsistency, pluck it out. You are not running a reform school or a social service agency."

"Inappropriate values" in management, he counsels, should be greeted with termination. His conviction is supported by research that indicates that just one bad apple in an organization can cause extraordinary amounts of grief. Consistent, and expensive, levels of staff turnover and underperformance can often be traced back to one misery-inducing executive who feels shielded by the organization from underlings. One of the reasons that physical shakeups of organizations (another high-performance management tool) are effective is that they help prevent fiefdoms and behavioural sinkholes from developing. But companies can be reluctant to move against problem managers because they overvalue their contribution and become concerned with severance costs, not appreciating the huge upside from allowing all the human capital being squandered by his or her behaviour to perform to their capabilities. "One change at a higher level can have an exponential impact," says Logan. "You can push a lot of paper around for a long time before you will have as much impact as one appropriate change will have."

"What's great about National Leasing is that its management doesn't just reward good performance: they call people on bad performance," says O'Grady. "People will do what they're rewarded for, but they'll also do what they're not reprimanded for." In other words, tolerating poor performance is a perverse sort of reward system: do things badly, and if we don't take you to task for it, you've been rewarded by being allowed to keep your job (and to be paid) for behaving or performing in what should be an unacceptable manner. "Companies need to look at what they're rewarding," says O'Grady, "because that affects culture. It's demoralizing if poor performers are compensated in the same way as good performers, and it's a tremendous motivator if good performance is recognized and celebrated. They're creating a favourable culture that way."

It may not be possible to say that there is a perfect corporate culture that suits all enterprises, but Logan believes there is a shared set of fundamentals that creates "a strong, enviable culture of high performance":

- *Understand long-term plans and communicate them to every person in the company:* "I know ours are communicated because I meet with all our departments and walk through the plans with them. Delegating communication doesn't work well. Our mission may be more complex than most, but it is certainly clear to everyone. Corporate goals are constantly being established and re-established, communicated, measured, and achieved. That is part of the culture. That leadership, combined with the attitude of employee ownership, tends to 'get things done.'"
- *Build a culture that includes everyone:* "Realistically, the top two-thirds of any organization will have the most impact. The bottom third is the newest, with the highest turnover and the least input, but it needs to be thoroughly captured."
- *Build your company for change:* "At National Leasing, people thrive on change and expect it." High-performance management companies revel not only in expecting the unexpected but in inciting it. Companies such as National Leasing have been inspired by dramatic turnaround case studies like that of New Zealand Post, the government-owned mail system that had to respond to orders to behave more like a private business. Among its many widely mimicked strategies was a policy of constant reorganization, which included reconfiguring the workplace layout in order to prevent bureaucratic stasis from setting in. National Leasing has adopted similar strategies. Logan relates how he had the company's eleven senior managers change the location of their offices. "Some of them moved a city block from where they were. Their first reaction was, 'That's nuts,' but now they see the value of moving, cleaning out the office, reorganizing as they move into the new digs, interacting with different people, and change itself. Now I am starting to see them moving mid-managers around."

Where National Leasing might depart from some of the general high-performance management theory is in Logan's provocative message of "We're not your employer for life." Job security guarantees are usually a key component of the employee "buy in" to this management system. But National Leasing is hardly promoting job insecurity in telling employees that the company should not be considered "employers for life." In fact, Logan's message is one of high employment security: by excelling at National Leasing, employees will be highly desired members of the workforce. "Our obligation to employees is that by having National Leasing on their resumé, they will be in demand."

Acknowledging that this message caused controversy, Logan emphasizes: "What I was really telling them was that we needed to prepare them for all options—a move inside or a move outside the company. Fortunately, we have been able to maintain a low turnover, but the fact is that we are making sure people are not afraid to move, and in fact expect to change."

- *Provide training, and more training:* "A relentless commitment to improving employees is a part of a great culture," Logan says. Businesses should ensure that employees "are improving themselves. Businesswise or personally, it does not matter necessarily how they are improving—just see that they are expanding their scope in some way. We even ran a program on dining etiquette. People taking courses tend to be mixing with a progressive crowd, and that's positive.
- *Respect each person's desire to do a good job, and give that person the opportunity to make a tangible contribution:* "If you expect high performance from your people, they need the right influences; they should not have obsolete equipment; they should not be housed in old-fashioned digs or be using rigid operat-

ing systems. If you find yourself caught with some of your support systems falling behind, set in motion a strategy to bring them back. Don't let your CFO freeze progress, just because he or she does not understand intangible investments. Manage assets and people the same way. Think quality, think long term, and think improving bit by bit."

- *Catch people doing things right, and then celebrate it:* "This can not be done too often. Canadians are far too modest and seem programmed to look for mistakes. We have a monthly meeting with the whole building where we try to capture successes."
- *Take time to shape an individual development plan for each employee:* "Each person has a job life cycle: first learning, then achieving, and then the true contributing, before the waning period. We have to enhance that employee's activities just before the waning sets in. That is the art of the game."
- *Employees must share in the company profits or have incentives:* The academic literature on high-performance management varies on what works best in compensation. Some think flat salaries are better than bonuses for inspiring teamwork. Some aren't sure that employee equity makes any difference to the company's profitability. National Leasing believes in employee equity. The company is entirely employee owned, and 82 percent of employees are shareholders. "Shareholders understand change and read plans a lot faster than staff do."
- *Above all else, focus on customers:* "Respect them, celebrate them, measure your response time to their needs. Get the leaders on a schedule to call customers on a weekly basis. Everyone in the company should be exposed to customers and make customer needs a priority."

The Deloitte perspective

Attracting and retaining talent to build an exceptional culture

Companies often view human resources as a sideshow to the main thrust of the business plan, with a short-term focus on filling job slots on an organizational chart. Nick Logan of National Leasing has recognized that attracting and retaining talent to build an exceptional culture is a strategic decision that is fundamental to his business's competitiveness.

Logan's company understands that attracting and retaining talent is critical to achieving sustained growth, and that National's main activity is not that of one business selling to or buying from another business: people sell to people, and if customers are to be valued, it follows that employees—the company's front line in the transactional process—need to be treated in exactly the same manner as customers.

National Leasing demonstrates the principle of valuing its employee team through monthly luncheons for all staff, during which financial results are shared, departmental successes in the market are highlighted, anniversaries of employee tenure are celebrated, and new staff are introduced. The office culture includes available workout rooms, billiard tables, an off-site conference retreat centre, and flexibility for work-at-home arrangements. The staff teams share in the company's victories and in return are committed to its future success.

Successful companies value their employees because valuable employees inevitably made them successful in the first place. And strength in employee ranks is not static.

Turnover is inevitable, and individual employees must have the opportunity to grow and improve—even to leave with a positive impression when their career goals can no longer be met.

A company's effort to create an employee-embracing culture can backfire if that embrace becomes smothering. When a business attempts to meet all aspects of an employee's life from vacations to the health club, what initially might seem like generosity on the part of the employer can begin to feel like a demand that an employee make an almost round-the-clock commitment to his or her place of work.

Which is not to say that these enhancements should not be offered. But companies with thriving and attractive corporate cultures such as National Leasing demonstrate that what is offered to an employee is not as important as how it is offered and why. National avoids any possibility of being overbearing in its embrace of employees because Logan and his team are not expecting to keep staff members forever. They are striving to train people who are strong in the employment market. And despite the wide variety of lifestyle benefits, there is a nice balance between establishing an office culture that is holistic to some degree and letting people drive their own involvement in it.

Career development within National is also very much controlled by the employee, and the offering plate is very broad. National has distinct business areas, and there is substantial cross-department transferring. People can move around in the organization to develop and broaden their skills, making them more marketable.

In the process, an employee develops a breadth of experience while the organization gains depth of talent. A particular division will not experience difficulties because one key person moves on. Other employees who have experience and understand that division can move in if necessary. A company is stronger when many employees have sound experience in different business areas.

Logan's approach to developing his talent infrastructure contains three main elements:

Plan for the long term:

- Understand and forecast the company's human resource needs.
- Develop the company's brand and message to build eminence and help draw the most attractive prospects.
- Implement a retention policy that influences who leaves and when.

Develop a motivational environment:

- Design creative and flexible compensation packages that satisfy employees and match with the company's labour-cost forecast.
- Manage the evolution of the organizational culture to ensure that employees have the power to innovate and make decisions.
- Provide ample opportunities for employees to grow, proposing multiple career paths, mentoring, and training.

Monitor progress and adapt:

- Implement performance measures to determine if the HR strategy is working toward achieving the corporate objectives and strategy.
- Benchmark the company against its competitors via formal satisfaction surveys and informal conversations with employees.
- Adapt to changes in the company and the talent pool.

Index

acquisitions, 29, 134–35, 137, 139, 151, 156–57, 159, 165, 172–73, 179, 223 (*See also* alliances)
action figures, 34, 39
Aecon Inc., 171
Agioritis, Gus, 54, 55, 63
Agreement on Internal Trade (1995), 125
Air Canada Centre (Toronto), 164
Air Hogs, xvii, 38, 41, 46
Aisenstat, David, 59
Albion Sands, 172
Alcohol and Gaming Commission (ON), 20
Alegría (Cirque du Soleil), 194
Alice Fazooli's! Italian Crabshack, 59
alliances, 20, 25, 27–51, 134–35, 137
ALS/2000 software, 133
Amarone-style VQA, 19, 22
Amazon.com, 140, 146, 149
AMC Theatres, 75
America Online, 141
André's (wines), 5, 10
Apple Inc., 29
application service provider (ASP) model, 95
AquaDodle, 24–25
Arby's, 66
Armadillo Texas Grill, 59
Armour, Angus, 137
Armour, Gordon, 122–23
Armour, Patricia, 123
Armour, Ralston, 137
Armour, Wesley, xvi, 123, 126, 127, 128, 131, 132, 134–35, 136–37
Armour Courier Service (ACS), 134–35
Armour Logistics Services (ALS), 133
Armour Transportation Systems, xiv, xvi, 122–39
Art Gallery of Ontario, 82
Ateliers (Cirque du Soleil studio), 194
Athens Games (2004), 82
Atlanta Games (1996), 82
AT&T, 141

Babies R Us, 32
Baie-Saint-Paul (QC), 192, 193
Barilko, Bill, 5
Barnum & Bailey circus, 189
Batman franchise, 39
BCE Place and Galleria (Toronto), 164
BCE Telecommunications, 95
Beatles show (Cirque du Soleil), 190, 194, 204–5
Bell Labs, 141
Bella Dancerella, 45–46
Bellagia hotel (Las Vegas), 191
Best Buy stores, 170
Best Managed program. *See* Canada's 50 Best Managed Companies awards program
big-box retailers, 32, 42
Black Diamond awards, 18
BlackBerry, 90
Blackmud Creek bridge (Edmonton), 170
Blain, Robert, 188, 194–95, 196, 198, 202
Blockbuster Video, 64

Blue Water Bridge, 164
BMO Computer Centre (Barrie, ON), 170
BMW, 29
Bobby's World (TV show), 70
bonding market, 89, 90
bootlegging, 10–11,12–13, 14 (*See also* home wine making)
Boston Bruins, 54, 55
Boston Chicken Inc., 64–65, 69, 72–73
Boston Market, 64, 65, 73–74
"Boston" name, trademark, 63–65, 72–74
Boston Pizza, xiv, xvii, 52–77
Boston Pizza International Ltd., 55, 64
Boston Pizza and Pasta, 54–55
Boston Red Sox, 63
Boston Seafood House Ltd., 64
Boston's the Gourmet Pizza, 75
Bradley, David, 125
brand definition, 201–6
brand extensions, 39, 45, 47, 202, 206–7
brand licensing alliances, 29, 33, 47
brand loyalty, 120
brand marketing, 67–68, 69, 71
brand mass, 69
brand promise, 106, 119
Breton, Patrice, 143, 158
Briggs, Bob, 132
Broker Forum, The, 148, 150, 151
Brown, Dwight, 163, 164, 174, 176
Bubba Gump Shrimp Company, 170
Bucyk, Johnny, 54, 55
Business Technology Solutions Award (2003), 216
business-to-business (BWB) environment, 143, 145, 146, 147–48, 151, 154, 155, 156
business-to-consumer environment, 145, 147
Butler, Mark, 132

California State University stadium, 164
CAMI (automotive plant), 82
Canada Life, 164
Canada Post, 20
Canada's 50 Best Managed Companies awards program, vii–viii, xiii–xiv, 89
Canadian Finance and Leasing Association (CFLA), 213
Canadian Information Productivity Awards (2003), 92
Canadian Marketing Hall of Legends, ix
Canadian National Railways (CN), 135
Canadian Tire, 170, 206
Canadian Trucking Alliance (CTA), 125, 126, 135
Canadian Trucking Alliance/Volvo Trucks Canada National Driver of the Year (2004), 131
Canadian War Museum, 162–63
Canadian Wine Institute, 13
Cara Operations Ltd., 60
Cargocan Logistics, 133
Carlo Fidani Peel Regional Cancer Centre, 170
Carnival Cruise Lines, 206
Caron, Guy, 188–89
Cartier, Jacques, 193
Cartier Inniskillin Vintners, 8
Casey's Bar & Grill, 60, 62
Catch-a-Bubble, 36–37
Cedar Lake Ensemble, 191
celebrities, marketing initiatives, 62–63, 69–70
Central Arizona Project water treatment plant, 170
Charal, 8
Cheers, 62, 63, 69
China, 25, 31, 55, 201
Chizick, Harold, 40, 42, 43, 47–48
Christmas season, 39, 43, 44
CIBC Commercial Banking, vii, viii
CIO Canada Award (2003), 92
Circus of China, 201
Cirque du Soleil, xiv, xvii, 185–210
Cirque du Soleil Fire Within, 207
Cirque du Soleil: 20 Years Under the Sun, 193, 201
Client Charter of Rights, 83
Cliff Clavin persona, 62–63, 69

Club des talons hauts, Le, 192, 193
coaching (employees),175, 210, 222
Code of Conduct, 83
Coleco, 38
collectibles: craze, 34, 40; market, 43, 45
commercials, 62–63
communication, effective (guiding principle), 178, 179–80
Complex Cirque, 198
concept restaurants, 59, 60 (*See also* theme restaurants)
continuous improvement, 98, 176–77, 181, 228
Cordoba, Mike, 56, 61–62, 66, 67, 69, 74, 75
core competencies, defining/leveraging, 128–32, 136–37, 138–39; expanding, 166
core values, 178, 181, 202, 203–4, 210, 225
Corel Centre (Ottawa), 163
corporate culture, xv, 216–33
corporate governance, 178–80
corporate ownership model, 57, 58, 59, 68, 74
corporation phase (org. structure), 182
Corteo (Cirque du Soleil), 191, 194, 195
Côté, Chantal, 199–200
Coté, Joe, 14
Coyle, Ron, 55
CQAT (PCL), 176
Crandon Park Golf Course (Key Bisayne, FL), 170
Credit Valley Hospital (Mississauga, ON), 170
cross-border trade, 10, 14, 135 (*See also* Free Trade Agreement; North American Free Trade Agreement)
cross-licensing, 39, 40
customer appreciation, 16, 110, 113, 118
customer base: aging, 114–15; demographics, 113–16; understanding, xv, 102–3, 108, 116, 127–28, 135
customer experience, 20, 23, 61–62, 113
customer loyalty, 16, 18, 71, 102, 103, 106, 108, 118, 120, 121, 130
customer privacy, 102
customer relationship management (CRM) software, 107–8, 109–13, 118, 119, 120
customer satisfaction, 102, 103, 106–7, 118, 119, 120 (*See also* satisfaction calls)
customer service, 100, 101, 103, 106, 118, 119, 120, 131–32, 135, 136, 137, 138, 229
Cyr, Mike, 62

Deloitte, vii, viii, xiii, xix; on alliances/acquisitions, 50–52; on finances, 159–61; on customer-centricity/sales/marketing; on designing orgs/growth; on employee retention/corporate culture, 230–33; on growth strategy, 22–23; on leadership/vision, 208–10; on risk management, 76–78; on technology solutions, 97–98; website, xix, 23
Deloitte & Touche (Montreal), 188
demand, creating, 116–18, 120–21
Denver International Airport, 171
deregulation, trucking industry, xvi, 123–27, 128, 129, 132, 135
Detroit Red Wings, 54
Di Zio family, 5–6, 11
Di Zio Magnotta, Rosanna, xvii, 3–23 (*See also* Magnotta, Gabe; Magnotta Winery)
Diamond "best in show" prize (2003), 92
Diefenbaker International Airport (Saskatoon), 171
Dieppe (NB), 122, 123
Dimnik, Tony, 57–58, 152–53, 157, 174, 176
discretionary spending, 117, 147, 148 (*See also* demand, creating)
Disney, 33, 34, 194, 204
diversification, 61, 123, 132–35, 138–39, 163, 165, 179, 215

diversity (guiding principle), 178
do-it-yourself wine market, 21 (*See also* home wine making)
Domain Name System, 144
dot.com boom/bust, 140, 142, 149, 152, 153, 155, 157, 220
Dow Chemical, 171
Dragone, Franco, 191, 201
Dralion (Cirque du Soleil), 194, 200–1
Driver of the Year (2004), 131
Duval, Pierre, 143, 158
Dylex, 104, 105, 106

earned media exposure, 46–47
Earth Buddy, 26–27
East Side Mario's, 59–60, 62, 71
Eaton's, 164
eBay, 40, 45
EdgeBuilder, 83, 86–90, 91–96, 97, 98
Edmonton (AB), 53, 54, 55 ,162, 170, 181, 224
Edmonton Flyers, 54
Edmonton International Airport, 171
Electronics ETO, 33
EllisDon, xv, 81–98
employee appreciation, 219–20, 229, 230–31
employee-ownership model, 167, 173–74, 181, 229
employee-supervisor relationship, 175
employee termination, 225–26
employee training, 175–76, 219, 228, 231
employees: Armour Trucking, 136–37, 138 (*See also* truck drivers); Boston Pizza, 71–72, 74; EllisDon, 82, 83, 91; Harry Rosen, 100, 106–7, 110, 111–13, 119, 120; National Leasing, 211–12, 217–32; PCL, 166, 168, 173–78
Enotrium, 19
Enron, 89
Equipment Leasing Association, 216
Esposito, Phil, 55
estate wineries, 9
Etch A Sketch, 33
ethnic communities (wine making), 6, 7, 10, 12–13
E*Trade, 155
expectation-setting, 225
Explorer browser, 141, 147
Expo '86 (Vancouver), 55

FAO Schwarz, 32
fast-food segment, 60
Federal Court of Canada, 64, 72
FedEx, 135, 137
Festa Juice Co. Ltd., 6–7, 9, 10, 12, 15
Fillion, Joanne, 201, 202, 203–4, 205, 206
financial ownership model, 57, 58–59, 68–69, 71, 72–73
Finding Nemo, 69
Fish, Peter, 36–37
Fisher-Klosterman, Inc., 172–73
Fleming, Bruce, 84, 85, 86, 87–89, 90, 91, 92, 93, 94, 95
flexibility, 134, 137, 210, 221, 230
focus groups, 26, 201
Ford Credit, 213
formative phase (org. structure), 181
Fox Television Network, 34, 70
free trade agreement (1989), 9–10, 125
Fuhrer, Dave, 25–26, 48
Funanuf, 25–26, 35, 41
Furby, 38

Gadbois, Denis, 142–43, 147, 149–51, 152, 154, 155, 157–58
Galarneau, Sylvie, 201
Gauthier, Daniel, 198, 202
Gehry, Frank, 82
General Motors, 82, 93
generalists, 29, 30
Georgian College (Barrie, ON), 91
gigantism, 165, 173
global positioning systems, 130
Global Restaurant Operations of Ireland Ltd., 65, 73–74
Globe and Mail, The, 14
Globe and Mail's Report on Business, 166
GMAC, 213

government e-tendering, 154
Greenspan, Alan, 140
Grieve, Ross, 167–70, 171, 173, 174–76, 179
growth, goal of, 164–68, 173
Growth Insights website (Deloitte), xix, 23
guiding principles statements, 178, 202

Halifax (NS), 75, 131–32, 169–70
Halifax Harbour Solutions Project, 169
Harary, Ronnen, 25, 26, 35, 37, 50
Harris, Jonathan, viii–ix
Harrison, George, 204
Harry Potter franchise, 40
Harry Rosen Inc., xvi, 99–121
Hasbro, 25, 35, 39
Heavy Construction News, 166
heavy industrial operations, 171–73
Hershey Foods, 35
high-performance management concept, 216–29
hobbyist specialties, 38
Hockey Night in Canada, 205
home meal replacement trade, 73
home wine making, 6–7, 12–13, 21
Honda, 93
honesty (core value), 178
Hong Kong, 36, 55
Hopkins, Garrett, 207
hospitality trade, 103
Hot Wheels, 33
hotel chains, 103
Hugo Boss, 116
Humber College, 20
humour, 219
Humphrey, Bob, 105
Hurricane Juan (2003), 131–32

IBM, 165
IBM Global Services, 95
Imaginarium, 32
implementation plan, 77, 78
imported wine, 9
incentives (employee), 219–20, 229
index cards, 109, 111
information age, 88
innovation, 137, 208
instincts, trusting, 26, 35, 43, 45–46
instruction-activity products, 45
integrity (core value), 178
Intel Corp., 154
intellectual property leveraging, 50
International Youth Year (1985), 193
internet, 83, 84–85, 88, 91, 130, 140–58, 215
internet protocol programming, 140
internet service provider (ISP), 143, 144
Interstate Commerce Commission (ICC), 124
InterVin International competition, 18
Intracom, 172
inventors, 35, 38, 40–42, 50
inventory management system (IMS), 44, 46, 47, 101, 102 (*See also* just-in-time inventory management)
IPO (initial public offering), 142, 149, 155, 152, 153–54, 159
iPod, 29
Irwin, Bryan, 36–37
Italian community (ON), 7, 12–13

Jack Astor's Bar & Grill, 59
Japan, 26, 41, 55; auto industry, 42; business models, 28
Java language, 154
job life cycle, 229
job security, 211–12, 228
Jurassic Park, 39
just-in-time inventory management, 101, 129–30

KÀ (Cirque du Soleil), 190, 194, 202, 203, 206
Kaburis, Mike, 75
KayBee Toys, 32
Keg, The, 59
Kelsey's Neighbourhood Bar & Grill, 60, 71
Key Royalties Income Fund, 59
KFC, 64
Kids R Us, 32

La Cité collégiale (Ottawa), 163
La Fête foraine, 192–93
La Nouba (Cirque du Soleil), 194
La Rêve (Cirque-like show), 191
label art, 19
Lake Winnipegosis retreat, 219–20, 222, 230
Laliberté, Guy, 187, 188, 190, 192–93, 198, 201, 202, 203, 206, 208
Lamarre, Daniel, 188, 190, 191, 197, 202, 206
Lantic Sugar, 132
Las Vegas, 187, 189, 190, 191, 192, 194, 197
LCBO, 3–5, 7–10, 11, 12, 13–14, 15, 16, 20–21, 22
Leaders in Management Education award, ix
leaders/leadership, 131, 135, 136, 137, 177, 208–9, 223–26
learning company, 180, 228 (*See also* continuous improvement)
Leblanc, Georges, 131
LeBreton Flats (Ottawa), 162
Legge, Karen, 217
Lego, 39
Lennon, John, 204
Lepage, Robert 202, 203
Les Échassiers de Baie-Saint-Paul, 192
less-than-load market (LTL), 135
licensing industry, 47
licensing tie-ins, 34, 39, 45, 47
lifestyle education, 221
Lin, Jackie, 36
Liquor Control Board of Ontario. *See* LCBO
Loblaws, 132
location (retailing), 99, 100, 104, 105
Logan, Nick, 212, 216–17, 219–21, 222–29, 230, 231
long-distance telephone market, 141
Lucent Technologies, 141

McCartney, Paul, 204
McDonald's chain, 33, 47, 64, 65, 73
McDonald's Restaurants of Canada, 73
McFlurry Maker, 47
McIntyre Arena (Schumacher, ON), 5
McIsaac, Frances, viii
McKids brand, 47
Maclean's magazine, ix
mad cow disease, 60
Magnotta, Gabe, xvi, 4, 5, 6, 7–23 (*See also* Di Zio Magnotta, Rosanne)
Magnotta Winery, 3–23
Mahovlich, Frank, 5
"make-goods," 103
Mall of America (Bloomington, MN), 170
Mandel, Howie, 69–71
market segmentation, 108
Marketing, 205
Marshmallow children's furniture, 41, 48
Marvel Comics, 34–35, 47
Mattel, 25, 33, 35, 39
Maxam Contracting Ltd., 171
media exposure, 46–47, 74
Mediagrif Interactive Technologies, xvii, 140–61
MEG (CA), 47
Melloy and Associates, 172
Melville, George, 55, 57, 77
Ménard, Renée-Claude, 192, 202, 205, 207
mentoring, 175, 210, 222
mergers, 165 (*See also* acquisitions; alliances)
Merrill Lynch Canada, 155
MERX electronic tendering system, 154
Mexican jumping beans, 46 (*See also* Mighty Beanz)
MGM Grand (Las Vegas), 190, 194
Microsoft, 141, 147, 174
Mighty Beanz, 43, 45, 47
Milestone's Grill & Bar, 60
Mirage (Las Vegas), 194
Mississauga (ON), 66, 67, 81, 170
mobility (guiding principle), 178
model aircraft sector, 38
module business, 172

Molson Inc., 201
Moncton (NB), 122, 123, 131, 135
Moncton Industrial Park, 126
Montana's Cookhouse, 60
Montreal, 141, 149, 155, 185, 188, 189, 194, 198, 206, 208
Moose Enterprises, 45
Moosehead beer, 134
Moriyama & Teshima Architects, 162
Mosaic browser, 144
motivational workplace, 217–33
Motor Carrier Act (1980), 124
Motor Traffic Act (1935), 124
Motor Vehicle Transport Act (1987), 125
Murray, Elspeth, 85–86, 88, 92, 95, 96, 127–28, 131, 135
mutual obligation (guiding principle), 178
Mystère (Cirque du Soleil), 191, 194, 199

Nadon, Judge Marc, 72
NASDAQ, 140, 153, 156
National Archives Gatineau Preservation Centre, 163
National Ballet of Canada, viii
National Circus School, 189
National Gallery of Canada, 82
National Hockey League (NHL), 45, 47, 54, 205
National Leasing, xiv, 211–33
National Post, vii, viii–ix
National Trade Centre (Toronto) 164
Nelson, Paul, 92
Nestlé, 48
Netscape Communications, 140–41, 144, 146–47
New York Festivals medal (1995), 207
New York, New York hotel (Las Vegas), 191
New York Toy Show, 37
New Zealand Post, 227
Niagara Peninsula, 8, 9, 18
Nickelodeon, 45
Nisku (AB), 171, 172
nontraditional toy market, 32
Nortel Networks, 141, 154
North American Free Trade Agreement (NAFTA), 125, 134
Nova Chemicals, 171
novelty, 33–34, 43, 143, 147
NPD Group, 32
Nunavut, 20

"*O*" (Cirque du Soleil), 191, 192, 194, 200, 205
O'Donnell, Rosie, 46–47
O'Grady, Shawna, 192, 198, 200, 218–19, 221–22, 225, 226
Ohio Arts, 33
oil and gas sector, 171, 173
oil sands boom, 171, 172
Olympics, 82, 190
Ontario wine industry, image, 9
opportunity, xv, xviii, 167, 168
organizational structure, 181–82
Orlando (FL), 187, 194, 204
Orr, Bobby, 55
Ottawa, 82, 162, 163, 164
Ottawa City Hall, 163
Outback Steakhouse, 60
ownership (guiding principle), 178

Pacinda, Mark, 66
panic buyers, 40
Parenting magazine, 25
Partners in Success (Treliving), 66
passion (core value), 178, 198, 222
payroll system (Cirque du Soleil), 196, 197
PCL College, 175–76
PCL Construction Group of Companies, xvii, 162–82
PCL Industrial Service Inc., 172
Pearson International Airport, 171
Pepsi International, 133–34
PepsiCo Restaurants International, 64
personal digital assistants (PDAs), 88, 90
Pet Rock, 27
Petropavlis, Chris, 53–54, 55, 63

pharmaceutical industry, 41
Pilot Ink Co., The, 25
pipe fabrication business, 171
Pizza Hut, 55, 60, 61, 64
Pizza Pizza, 61
Platinum Club, ix, 166
Playskool, 33
Plunkett, Stephen, 62, 63, 66, 67–68, 70, 71
PoleStar, 134
Poole, Ernest, 166
Poole, George, 166
Poole, John, 166
pop-culture brands, 34, 39
Popular Science, 38
premium wines, 17–19, 21
President's Choice, 206
pricing system, wines, 13–16, 17
Prime Restaurants, 59–60
profit-sharing, 229 (*See also* employee-ownership model)
P-3 (public-private partnership), 169
Public Archives building (Ottawa), 162

Queen's School of Business, vii, ix, xiii, 12, 26, 57, 86, 106, 127, 152, 174, 192, 218
QUEST initiative (PCL), 176–77, 178, 181
Quidam (Cirque du Soleil), 194

Rabie, Anton, 25, 26, 34, 35, 36–37, 45, 50
radio frequency identification (RFID), 96, 102
radio-controlled (RC) model aircraft, 38
Rapport Dialup Switch (Nortel), 141
Ratzenberger, John, 62–63, 69, 70
RCMP, 55, 66
recession (early 1990s), xviii, 8, 14, 55, 84, 105, 129, 167
recreational marine industry, 114
Reimer, 135, 137
reorganization, 182, 227
reporting systems, 85, 88 (*See also* EdgeBuilder)
resale boat market, 114
resources sector, 171–72
respect, 137, 176, 177, 178, 228–29
retreat centre, off-site, 219–20, 222, 230
rewards (employees), 226, 230
Rhinoceros Party, 192
Richard Ivey School of Business, 26
Ringling Bros. Circus, 189
risk assessment, 77, 78, 180
risk management, 76–78, 197
risk-taking, 43, 51
Robertson, Russ, viii
ROE (return on equity), 224, 225
Rogers Centre (Toronto), 82
Rosen, Harry, 100, 104, 108, 119 (*See also* Harry Rosen Inc.)
Rosen, Larry, xvi, 100, 104–5, 109, 110, 111, 115, 116, 117–18, 119
Ryerson School of Business, 170

safety (guiding principle), 178
St. Elsewhere, 69, 70
St. Hubert Chicken, 60, 75
St. Lucia, 89–90
Ste-Croix, Gilles, 192
SalesLogix, 109, 112–13
Saltimbanco (Cirque du Soleil), 194, 207
Sam Malone character *(Cheers),* 63
SARS, 60
Saskatchewan Indian Federated College, 163
satisfaction calls, 109, 113, 121, 229 (*See also* customer service)
Sawchuk, Terry, 54
Sawka Group, 215
Schulich School of Business, viii
Scotia Plaza (Toronto), 164
Sears, 32
Seattle-Tacoma International Airport, 171
Securitization Administration System, 215–16
September 11, 2001, 60, 89, 135
Sesame Street, 39, 46
Shanahan,Wayne, 74–75

Shell Chemicals, 155
Shrinky Dinks, xvii, 34
Siegfried and Roy, 189
Sikorsky helicopters, 170
Simpsons, The, 39, 47
SIR Corp., 59, 60
Six Easy Steps to Making Wine the Festa Way (Di Zio Magnotta), 7, 11
SkyDome, 82
Smith, David Ellis, 81–82
Smith, Donald J., 81–82, 83, 85, 86, 87–88, 90–92, 94, 95
Smith, Geoff, xv, 81, 82, 90
S'Mores Maker, 35, 47
social responsibility (guiding principle), 178
Special Occasions Permit, 6
specialists, 30
specialty children's channels, 45
specialty wine products, 19
Spence, Don, 55
Spencer Francey Peters (branding agency), 205
spending profiles, 112
Spin Master Ltd., xvii, 24–51
SpongeBob SquarePants, 34
sports bars, 61, 71
Squishee Maker, 47
stabilization phase (org. structure), 182
Standing Committee on General Government (ON), 10
Stanley, Allan, 5
Star Wars franchise, 33, 39
Starr, Ringo, 204
Stasiuk, Vic, 54
Stink Blasters, 47
Strategic Council (marketing firm), 205
succession planning, 137, 175
Suncor Energy, 171, 172
supermarkets, 10, 16
Superstore, 132
supervisory training, 175–76
Surface Transportation Board (US), 124
Suzuki, 82
Swiss Chalet, 60, 61
Syncrude, 172
table wines, 14, 17
takeout and delivery operations, 61, 73
Target, 32, 46
target-market opportunities, 120–21, 132–33
teamwork (guiding principle), 178
Ted Baker (clothing line), 116
Teenage Mutant Ninja Turtles, 34
Telecom Act (1996), 141
Télémagik Productions, 207
television marketing, 62–63
Tengamo, 44
test marketing, 44, 45
Teton Industrial Construction, 173
T.G. Bright winery, 8
theme restaurants, 170
Thibault, Claude, 155, 156–57
Tickle Me Elmo, 37, 46–47
Tidball, George, 59
Tim Hortons, 53, 206
Tip Top Tailors, 104
Tokyo Disney Resort, 187, 194, 204
Toronto Eaton Centre, 164
Toronto Star, 14
Toronto Stock Exchange (TSX), 5, 154, 155
total quality management (TQM), 216
Tower, Larry, 132
toy industry, 31–35 (*See also* Spin Master Ltd.)
Toy Industry Association, 32, 35
toy retailers, 42–45
Toys R Us, 32
Toy Story, 69
trademark protection, 63–65, 72–74
Trade-marks Opposition Board, 73
traditional toy market, 31, 34
training, 175–76, 219, 228, 231
travel, post 9/11, 60, 89
Treasure Island (Las Vegas), 194
Treliving, Jim, 55, 57, 66, 75, 77
Triple Thick Milkshake Maker, 47
truck drivers, 128–32, 136–37
trust, 137, 176, 177

Ultimate Toy Award, 35
underperformance (employee), 225–26
Université du Québec à Montréal, 142
University of New York, 66
University of Western Ontario, 26, 105

Value Plus Program, 215
value-management process, 176–78
values, inappropriate, 225–26
Vancouver International Airport, 171
Varadi, Ben, 25, 26, 50
Varekai (Cirque du Soleil), 194
Vaughan (ON), 3, 8, 20
venture capital (VC), 149–52, 153, 159
Versace, 116
video games, 31
Vincor International, 5, 8, 10
Vineyards Estate Wines (outlets), 10
Vintages (LCBO outlets), 20, 21
Vintners Quality Alliance Act, 9
vision, 178, 187, 201, 202, 206, 208, 209, 210
Vision Mobile, 92
VQA, 9

Wal-Mart, 32, 46, 53, 191
Walt Disney World Resort, 187, 194
Walton, Michael, 132
Walton, Nancy, 191
warehousing, 133
warranties, 103
Western Hockey League, 54
WestJet, 206
Whitbread PLC, 59
Wild, Wild West, 39
Windjammer Landing resort (St. Lucia), 89–90
Windows 95, 141
Wine Council of Ontario, 10, 12, 14
wine snobbery, 15, 18
WineRack (outlets), 10
winery stores, 9–10, 15, 19–20
Winnie the Pooh (Disney), 33, 39
Wong, Ken, ix, 12, 16, 18, 26, 44–45, 46, 48–49, 106, 109, 110, 113
work hours, flexible, 221
work-from-home capabilities, 221, 230
work/life balance, 221, 222, 230
workout rooms, 221, 230
workplace: celebrations, 229, 230; fun, 219–21; motivational, 217–33
World Exchange Plaza (Ottawa), 163
World Wide Web, 140, 143, 144
Worlds Apart, 41
Wynn, Steve, 191

Xerox Leasing, 213

Yellow Submarine, 190, 204–5
Young, Cynthia, 17, 19
Y2K, 214
Yu-Gi-Oh!, 41, 45

Zegna Sport, 113
Zumanity (Cirque du Soleil), 191, 194, 205